THOMAS MORE
ESSAYS ON THE ICON

THOMAS M·O·R·E
ESSAYS ON THE ICON

Edited by
Damian Grace and Brian Byron

DOVE COMMUNICATIONS
MELBOURNE.

Published by
DOVE COMMUNICATIONS PTY LTD
60—64 Railway Rd, Blackburn, Victoria 3130, Australia

Cover design by Lynne Muir
Typeset by Dove Communications
Printed in Australia by Globe Press, Fitzroy
© copyright 1980 Damian Grace and Brian Byron
All rights reserved.
No part of this book may be reproduced without permission in writing from the publishers.

National Library of Australia
Cataloguing in Publication data

Thomas More, essays on the icon.

   Six essays presented at the Thomas More Quincentenary Conference, Sydney, August 1978.
   ISBN 0 85924 156 4.

   1. More, Sir Thomas, Saint—Addresses, essays, lectures. 2. Christian saints—England—Addresses essays, lectures. I. Grace, Damian. II. Byron, Brian. II. Thomas More Quincentenary Conference, 1978, Sydney, N.S.W.

942.05'2'0924

FOREWORD

In August 1978 the Thomas More Quincentenary Committee sponsored a three-day conference at St John's College in the University of Sydney as part of celebrations to mark the five-hundredth anniversary of More's birth. Sixteen Australian scholars were joined by Father Bernard Bassett S.J. from London and Abbe Germain Marc'hadour of the Universite Catholique de l'Ouest, Angers, France, in presenting papers of a range and variety to match the many-sidedness of their subject. This volume offers a selection from that occasion together with an essay by Professor Marc'hadour delivered on the eve of the conference as the Sir Charles McDonald Lecture.

Essays on the Icon is a fitting title for these studies of More. His strength of character has inspired four centuries of rich iconography, from the paradigmatic Holbein portrait to the sculptural essays of Joly and Bevis and the cinematic realization of Fred Zinnemann. Precisely because they are objects of veneration, however, icons are also the targets of iconoclasts fearful that the precious image may obscure or distort reality. In More's quincentennial year, Australian scholars were fortunate to hear Professor Geoffrey Elton present a different portrait of the man, a vision of the reality behind the image, 'The Real More'. The present papers are offered in the same spirit of criticism and reappraisal, yet this critical scrutiny serves to enhance rather than alter the traditional picture. In particular, More's religious commitment, lately the subject of revisionism, is reasserted here by Dr Purcell and Dr Byron, even as Father Minns shows him to have been too zealous at times in controversy. More's combative image as controversialist is softened, however, in Abbe Marc'hadour's essay on his gift for the give-and-take of genuine conversation. Tony Cousins's paper on More as English poet illuminates a neglected aspect of his work. Finally, Averil and Conal Condren examine the legend of More, the subject and the product of much iconography. But if myth attached itself early to his memory, then that myth may be read not only as an indication of the needs and fancies of his devotees, but also as token of his fitness as a mythopoeic figure.

The editors are grateful to the sponsors of the Sir Charles McDonald Lecture, Sancta Sophia and St John's Colleges within the University of Sydney, and the Newman Graduate Association, and to the organizer of the Lecture, Fr Gregory Meere, for permission to publish Professor Marc'hadour's address. We are grateful also for the assistance given by Fr J. Reinberger, former Rector of St John's, and his staff; for financial support from the British Council and the New South Wales government; and for secretarial help from the Department of Adult Education of the University of Sydney. The chairman of the Quincentenary Committee, the Hon. Mr Justice Slattery, merits our special thanks for his untiring efforts to make the conference a success. To Mrs Chryss Grindrod, who willingly found time in a busy schedule to type manuscripts and make corrections, we are most grateful.

As this volume was going to press news came of the untimely death of Sister Purcell. Her critical mind and congenial company will be much missed by her friends and fellow students of medieval and early modern Europe.

D. G.
B. B.

CONTENTS

Here I Sit: Thomas More's Genius for Dialogue
Germain Marc'hadour — 9

St Thomas More as English Poet
A.C. Cousins — 43

Through a Needle's Eye: Thomas More The Wealthy Saint
Brian Byron — 53

Thomas More's Use of Scripture in *The Dialogue Concerning Heresies*
Denis P. Minns — 71

Dialogue of Comfort for Whom?
Maureen Purcell — 89

More and Sokrates: The Limits of Comparison and Symbolic Potency
C. and A.C. Condren — 109

HERE I SIT: THOMAS MORE'S GENIUS FOR DIALOGUE
G. MARC'HADOUR

To portray Martin Luther, Professor Bainton of Yale University chose for his title the answer that the Saxon monk is reported to have given to the Emperor Charles V and the German dukes when he appeared before them at the Diet of Worms, in April 1521: 'Here I stand.' An excellent title for an excellent evocation of the mighty challenger that Luther was.[1]

I suggest 'Here I sit' as an equally felicitous phrase to sum up the personality, the mental and spiritual likeness of St Thomas More. Hans Holbein has not only caught More's features but his natural posture when he portrays him seated on a bench, sharing the cushioned bench with his father, Sir John, who was a judge of the King's Bench, no idle play on words. The precious pen-and-ink sketch of the Chelsea household affords our only full view of Thomas More, including his feet in their flat-soled sandals firmly planted on the floor. There is a footstool a few inches away, provided (it would seem) for him or for his father, but these earthy lawyers and magistrates appear to prefer direct contact with the ground. The feet of Sir Thomas are wide apart, as if he were imitating his master Henry VIII. He sits gazing idly in front of him, his rather coarse hands buried in his wide sleeves. Most of the children in the picture stand, as does the fool Harry Patenson. Margaret and Cecily sit on their heels, or perhaps on low stools concealed by their skirts. Lady Alice alone is shown kneeling, but one can imagine Sir Thomas vetoing the position: Holbein's own hand says in the margin, in German, 'This one shall sit.' Thus we know that, in the final portrait, now lost, the housewife was seated like her husband.

The tradition has been respected by the best of modern sculptors, notably by L. Cubitt Bevis in the impressive larger-than-life bronze statue of More that was unveiled at Chelsea on 21 July 1969 by the Speaker of the House of Commons. Here, too, More sits with clasped hands, his face tipped slightly to the left, looking in the direction of Westminster, the City, the Tower, and beyond, where the tidal river loses itself into the salt main. 'I seated More', Mr Bevis said to me when I visited him, 'since this was a characteristic pose whether as philosopher, Speaker of the House of Commons, Judge, Lord Chancellor, or in his Chelsea home surrounded by his family.'

Hans Holbein's sketch of the Chelsea household has been likened by art historians to the Italian compositions known as *Conversazione*. Now, what is a literary dialogue except conversation as reported and stylized by a writer? The exchange of words being basic to human communication, dialogue was bound to be as old a genre as literature itself. It enlivens the Bible, for instance, right from chapter 3 of Genesis, where the first human couple talk not only together, but with their Maker, and with their foe the serpent. The Book of Job, of course, is a marvellous dialogue, with a great variety of interlocutors, from God and Satan to Job's nagging wife and burdensome comforters.

In that great tradition Thomas More has a conspicuous place. Among the books that stand out in More's literary production as indubitable masterpieces are his three Dialogues. The *Utopia*, written over the years 1515–16 in Latin, was his first composition of any length to appear in the language. *A Dialogue concerning Heresies and Matters of Religion*, published in June 1529, was the first and the best of More's seven polemical works in the English language. *A Dialogue of Comfort Against Tribulation*, written in the Tower and piously kept in manuscript by the family, was rushed into print as soon as Mary Tudor succeeded as Queen; it appeared in 1553, and was the first dated book to issue from the press of Richard Tottel. Thus *dialogue* is the first word in the titles of More's first works as an apologist for the faith, and then as a prisoner for the faith.

These major works must not conceal other expressions of More's genius for dialogue. According to Erasmus, 'while still young, he composed a dialogue in which he defended Plato's communism'.[2] Drama is the scion of colloquy, and we know, again through Erasmus, that young More 'wrote plays and acted them';[3] none is known to have survived, though one title, *Solomon*, is mentioned in a letter of More's youth.[4] More's extempore acting as a page in Lambeth was among the signs of promise that delighted Archbishop Morton.[5] His genius as a playwright appears in most of his works, from the farcical *Merry Jest* of the policeman disguised as friar[6] to the *Dialogue of Comfort*, from which I shall excerpt for you a *prima facie* segment, rather undramatic, since it deals with dreaming. Old Antony, in search of criteria whereby to discern 'God's true revelation' from 'the devil's false delusion', suggests a difference similar to that between 'the sight of a thing while we be waking and... while we dream thereof'. His nephew Vincent likes the 'pretty similitude' and concludes that discernment is 'easy'.

Antony: Not so easy, cousin, as you ween it were. For how can you now prove unto me that you be awake?
Vincent: Marry, lo, do I not now wag my hand, shake my head, and stamp with my foot here in the floor?
Antony: Have you never dreamed ere this that you have done the same?
Vincent: Yes, that have I, and more too than that.[7]

No stage indications are needed for young Vincent's gestures punctuating his vivid philosophical discussion in the sick-room of his old kinsman.

The Business of Communication
If literary dialogue, under its Greek name, is but the artistic development of spoken conversation, and if Thomas More was both a fine artist and a great conversationalist, one would expect him to enjoy dialogue, to try it as a vehicle for his message, and to do a good job of it. The store he set by oral communication appears from the time he found—which means the time he made—for conferring with his household. In an oft-quoted letter of 1516 to Peter Giles, printed among the prefaces to *Utopia*, the very busy lawyer, under-sheriff and

diplomat apologizes for having been so slow in finishing his *opusculum*. He enumerates the multifarious demands of his legal business, and continues:

> When I return home from a day's work, I must talk with my wife, chat with my children, and converse with my servants. All this activity I reckon and account among business since it must be done, and done it must be unless a man wants to be a stranger in his own home.[8]

The addressee of these lines was Giles, or Gillis, 'greffier'—that is, town clerk—of Antwerp, whose 'charming conversation'[9] More, in the very text of *Utopia*, credits with dispelling much of his own homesickness. Conversing with like-minded people was, Erasmus tells us, the recreation most prized by his London friend. (Allen 4, ep. 999)

As a young man, More had tried the austerities of the Charterhouse, and had not been put off by such penances as fasting, long vigils, the scourge and the hairshirt; but we may safely guess that if he never considered becoming a Carthusian monk himself, it was on account of the harshest deprivation, company. Since he married eventually because 'he could not shake off the desire for a wife', as Erasmus puts it (Allen 4, ep. 999), how could he have vowed a lifetime of total solitude?

Thirty years later, when Henry VIII gave him a cell in the Tower, he was true to his early sociable self. He did 'not mislike' prison fare: 'whenever I complain', he merrily said to the Lieutenant, 'then thrust me out of your doors' (Roper, p. 77/20). He welcomed the coarse food, the scant daylight, the cold, the filth, 'the mice and rats' mentioned with a shudder by his wife (Roper, p. 82/17). Among his true ordeals, next to the heart's agony caused by the high displeasure of his sovereign lord, was the lack of genuine conversation. One of the graces he begs for in the litany that we are privileged to have in his own handwriting is 'To be content to be solitary' (*CW* 13, p. 226/9). 'Content', as I think I could prove statistically, is a weaker epithet in More's vocabulary than 'glad' and 'joyful', which also occur in this prayer.[10] It bespeaks acceptance, resignation. Perhaps no man ought to aspire to facing loneliness joyfully, since the Son of Man was not able to bear it in the Garden of his Agony. And whereas the prisoner lustily retorts to Dame Alice's evocation of the amenities of Chelsea —the 'right fair house, library, gallery, orchard' (Roper, p. 83/1)—he confesses in a letter to Margaret that he misses the chance of chatting with the family:

> Nor never longed I, since I came hither, to set my foot in mine own house, for any desire of, or pleasure of my house, but gladly would I sometime somewhat talk with my friends, and specially my wife and you that pertain to my charge. (Rogers, p. 543/140f.)

In the next—the farewell—paragraph comes an enumeration yet more detailed than that in the preface to *Utopia*, because the writer has meanwhile become the head of a larger, truly patriarchal community:

> And thus, mine own good daughter, have me recommended to my good bedfellow and all my children, men, women and all, with all your babes and your nurses and all the maids and all the servants, and all our kin, and all our other friends abroad. And I beseech Our Lord to save them all and keep them. And I pray you all pray for me, and I shall pray for you all. (Rogers, p. 544/158f.)

Thus prayer achieves, on a higher level, what physical presence no longer can; nor does the merriness preached by the martyr to all his correspondents owe anything to make-believe, or to a Stoic defiance of fortune: it rests on a shared expectation of heaven, where, he writes to Antonio Bonvisi, 'we shall need no letters, where no wall shall dissever us, where no porter shall keep us from talking together'.[11]

Conferring with one's fellow man is seen, not only as a duty, but as a thing of pleasure both here and in eternity. It attains that high point of perfection defined by Horace as 'blending the useful with the sweet'—*miscuit utile dulci*. The sweetness it affords comes of course from its very naturalness.

Montaigne agrees with Erasmus and More when he writes: 'Le plus fructueux et naturel exercice de notre esprit, c'est à mon gré la conférence.'[12]

Conference—a good enough term for a transition from the chitchat of informal encounters to the studied communication that could easily crystallize into a formal dialogue. And thus we return to the three peaks of More's literary accomplishment.

The Semi-Dialogue of 1516: Utopia

Utopia is a dialogue only in its first, less Utopian, book. There the English diplomat, with a family of four children aged between six and eleven, on the eve of accepting full involvement in public affairs, listens to a seasoned Portuguese seafarer, who is a bachelor and a bit of a doctrinaire, a preacher of abstention and detachment. The first page, which introduces all three characters, is such a delightful vignette-cum-dialogue that, although you have all read it, some of you in the Latin original, I beg your permission to read it out again.

> (On my way home from church I caught sight of Peter Giles) in conversation with a stranger, a man of advanced years, with sunburnt countenance and long beard and cloak hanging carelessly from his shoulder. His appearance and dress seemed to me to be those of a ship's captain.
> When Peter had espied me, he came up and greeted me. As I tried to return his salutation, he drew me a little aside and, pointing to the man I had seen him talking with, said:
> — Do you see this fellow? I was on the point of taking him straight to you.
> — He would have been welcome, said I, for your sake.
> — No, said he, for his own, if you knew him. There is no mortal alive today who can give you such an account of unknown people and lands—a subject about which I know you are always greedy to hear.
> — Well, then, said I, my guess was not a bad one. The moment I saw him, I was sure he was a ship's captain.
> — But you are quite mistaken, said he, for his sailing has not been like that of Palinurus but that of Ulysses or, rather, of Plato. (CW, 4 p. 48/18f.)

Notice that the 'dress and appearance' of Raphael Hythlodaeus are those of a role, of a type, rather than an individual. Faced with this combination of Ulysses and Plato, plus a biblical dimension suggested by the man's first name, Morus will not say much. When he first breaks his dutiful silence, it is to lodge his famous plea for involvement; Hythlodaeus has finished proving that there is no room for philosophy in the courts of princes, and Morus replies:

> True enough, no room for this academic philosophy which thinks that everything is suitable everywhere. But there is another, a more civil philosophy, which knows its stage, adapts itself to the play in hand and performs its role neatly and appropriately . . . Whatever play is being performed, perform it as best you can, and do not upset it all simply because you think of a more interesting one. So it is in the commonwealth. So it is in the counsels of monarchs . . (CW4, p. 98/10f.)

The major dialogue of *Utopia* is between two voices within More himself, even where it compares England with Nowhere. On this specific issue, the voice that prompted Thomas More to say 'yes' to the king and to climb on to the stage of Tudor statecraft, knowing it to be a scaffold too, won the contest; yet it never drowned the warning Erasmian voice, which deprecated futile entanglements, and held him back from being sucked into the maelstrom of activism, and from sacrificing to the political idol—expediency. He embraced Martha without rejecting Mary's better part.[13]

Nor did 'the proof of the pudding' alter his mind perceptibly. After twelve years of public engagement, having risen to the position of Chancellor of the Duchy of Lancaster, he handles the young Messenger in his 1529 *Dialogue* in terms reminiscent of those of Hythlodaeus that I have just quoted. When the Messenger, in a discussion about judiciary evidence, imagines a trial at which all the sworn witnesses, however many they may be, perjure themselves, 'the author' does not dismiss the wild surmise, but says:

Your case, though it be possible, were rather to be granted at a school in argument than at a court in judgement. (*D.C.H.*, III, 5; *EW*, p. 215f)

The *philosophia scolastica* and *philosophia civilior* are cruxes for translators—would they could be rendered into rhythmic, formulaic, truly oral English like their semantic near-equivalents. In the sentence I have just read out, the phrase 'at a school in argument' balances 'at a court in judgement', especially if one keeps in mind that early Tudor pronunciation gave 'judgement' three syllables.

Short of the capacity to emulate and equal the original, we should at least learn from More some elementary rules of dialogue, and one is the economy he uses for the link-words. In his *Dialogue Concerning Heresies*, the alternation between More and his young interlocutor is indicated by an endless repetition of 'quod I' and 'quod he'. Lesser writers, possessed by an itch for variety, had an easy task deriding More's 'dialogue of quod he and quod I'. More retorts that such tags are inevitable 'in the rehearsing of a communication had between myself and another man'.[14] He might have added that all the masters of the genre use a similar economy, from Plato and the Bible to the born story-tellers of our day. In that other masterpiece of 'dialogue d'idées', Voltaire's *Candide*, you have 'dit Candide' flatly alternating with 'dit Martin'; the unobtrusive proclitic monosyllables leave the mind free to dwell upon the matter under discussion, free and alert to catch the pregnant puns and loaded allusions. In the first page of *Utopia*, which I read to you a few minutes ago, Father Surtz wisely echoes More's *inquam/inquit* with 'said I' and 'said he'; he refrains from carving these pegs. But in the last pages of Book I, where *inquit* occurs six or seven times and *inquam* four or five times, the translator launches into an exercise in *copia verborum*, which is incongruous because no *copia rerum* justifies it. You have 'he rejoined', 'I declared', 'he commented', 'I ventured', 'objected Peter', 'he countered', 'he replied', 'I suggested', so that, after these eight verbs, one is relieved to find at last 'said I', reflecting More's own simple *inquam*.[15] The effect is perhaps more ludicrous in the telescoping of my comment, but do read the passage with 'said I' and 'said he', or 'quoth I' and 'quoth he', and you will agree that the translator should have spared himself all that laborious elaboration. You may, I said, try *'quoth I'* and *'quoth he'*, but don't, please, if it is for quaintness' sake, because Thomas More was anything but quaint![16]

A Dialogue Concerning Heresies (1529)
And thus we turn firmly toward the book of 'quod he and quod I', which is more truly a dialogue than *Utopia*, and which we can enjoy in More's own English. Because it has a long title, which reads like 'an advertisement' (de Winton), or like a menu if you wish, it has gone under several short-titles. The Yale edition, following the Rastell folio of 1557, calls it *A Dialogue concerning Heresies*.[17] More himself invariably refers to it as 'my dialogue', as if to indicate that the manner is not less important than the matter, that the spirit of friendly exchange counts as much as the topics to be threshed together. Indeed the form[18] imparts to the work a unity of atmosphere that is the more precious because of the variety of topics.

This is the only dialogue in which More treats himself to the leading role. I quoted him a while ago describing it as 'a communication had between myself and another man'. Is this 'self' a closer likeness of him than the Morus of *Utopia*? The Chancellor of the Duchy of Lancaster could not tamper with his identity as freely as the diplomat of thirteen years earlier. The mere fact that he is known personally to a high percentage of his prospective public forces him to achieve a lifelike self-portrait. The location of the discussion is his own house at Chelsea. His wife comes twice into the picture, once as the hostess whose dinner is getting cold, once as popess in the reformist imagination of More's young interlocutor. Old Sir John More is featured at least four times. He is well-known and well-liked in the London of the Inns of Court, of Parliament, even of the King's Council. His successive marriages have multiplied his connections. Also, while Sir John lives and laughs, Sir Thomas, though a senior minister of the Crown, remains 'young More', which is something of an asset in the debate he is holding with the younger generation. Dame Alice, too, is an asset, given the day's rampant anticlericalism: marrying her has, as it were, wedded More indissolubly to the lay state, since, as he says himself, a twice-married man, even if he becomes a widower, is ineligible for holy orders. Other elements of realism, which are assets too, are More's references to his business at court, to his links with the City, for instance his pre-Chelsea days as parishioner of Saint-Stephen's, and his judiciary experience, especially in connection with the Hunne affair. He makes direct capital of his wide range of travelling contacts and his extensive reading:

> The places where myself hath been, with common report of other honest men, from all other places of christendom, but by books also, and remembrances left of long time ... (1, 2; *EW*, p. 113)

The only make-up at More's disposal is of the kind used in a television studio to counteract or temper the cruel searching of the limelight, and thereby restore rather than alter the speaker's features. More plays his own self with the mastery of a born and trained actor. The range of his voice is wide enough for him to be able to select some intonations and still sound authentic. Like Socrates, he can be now gadfly, now midwife. He unmasks intellectual fraud, exposes the cheapness of fashionable slogans, patiently qualifies and gives nuance to the crude simplifications. He is also the pious maintainer of the legal, cultural and spiritual bonds that bind our today to an unbroken line of yesterdays.

Within the book, however, More's name is never used. Only on the title-page is it given as 'Sir Thomas More Knight', the first public use More makes of a title bestowed on him in 1521. His interlocutor, also nameless, consistently addresses him as 'Sir', which has manifold appositeness coming to a knight from a young man who could be his son and who poses as his pupil. In having no name by which to call his guest, the author differs from the historic More, who, judging from his letters and his son-in-law's memoir, was fond of personal vocatives— 'Son Roper', 'Mine own good daughter', 'Margaret', 'Meg', 'Mrs Alice' and so on. The forfeiting of names in this exchange has the virtue of turning the dialogists into types: the middle-aged magistrate and paterfamilias sits face-to-face with the half-unattached bachelor and private tutor. The visitor has come to Chelsea, the preface tells us, on behalf of his master, a 'worshipful friend' of More's, who lives somewhere in the provinces. He is the bearer of a 'letter of credence' asking More to answer any question he raises. Still fresh from the University,[19] he is tempted by some of the new ideas. He has orders to be bold in expressing his doubts and grievances, and in voicing an assortment of complaints he has heard from others. He lashes freely at England's clergy, who brand as heretical all true preaching of the Gospel, and burn the New Testament truly englished by Tyndale, while they encourage for lucre's sake popular superstitions fed by pilgrimages and their sham miracles, spurious relics, saint-worship, which robs Christ of his place as only Advocate, and image-worship, which is plain idolatry.

These and suchlike topics are threshed out in four long sessions—two forenoons in More's study, two afternoons 'in an arbour', with a fortnight's interval during which the Messenger returns to the University and tries More's answers on his friends there. Having recorded the debate in writing, More sends the book to his 'worshipful friend' with a letter answering the initial letter of credence.

This epistolary framework, broad and elastic, which More had already used to package his *Utopia* and his 1523 *Responsio ad Lutherum*, invites us to keep in mind the bond of double friendship that binds the interlocutors together and to their common friend, never seen as an actor, but ever present as the sponsor of the encounter and the addressee of the proceedings—the phrase 'quod he' is not seldom replaced by 'quod your friend'.

The exchange begins abruptly in chapter I when the Messenger protests at the restrictions imposed by the clergy on scriptual literature, 'as though it were heresy for a christian man to read Christ's gospel'. To the insular bones of contention he musters he soon adds an ominous name—Luther. Since he is also spokesman for the laity at large, we cannot quite assess his own religious stance. Our initial distrust evaporates when his sense of humour, duly mentioned in the letter of credence, comes to the fore, and shows him to resemble More, not Tyndale. He has been instructed to beware of his Chelsea host:

> Ye use (my master saith) to look so sadly when ye mean merrily, that many times men doubt whether ye speak in sport when ye mean good earnest. (I, 6, *EW*, 127. B)

'The injection of this ambiguity at this point in the discourse seems deliberate' (Schaeffer, p. 139). The Messenger himself is less of a dry joker, his youthful ardour carries him away, but the cheerful ring and spirited audacity of his verbal assaults make More augur well of his actual behaviour: 'Well, quod I, ye speak merrily, but I wote well ye will do better, whatsoever ye say' (I, 15, *EW*, p. 136 H). So we have ambiguity compounded. But the conditions exist for true communication. We witness, says W. Gordon, 'the cogs of two different yet cognate minds, engaging each other'. The young man's creed is rather tentative and fluid, and this alone saves him from being a heretic. The heretic, by definition, has chosen,[20] and clings to his choice, so he 'could almost be defined as one with whom dialogue is impossible' (Schaeffer, p. 115). This is illustrated in the chapter (IV, II) where a 'not unlearned' preacher is being harried in vain by the toreros of Catholic orthodoxy — 'a kind of anti-dialogue within a real dialogue' (Schaeffer, p. 196), whereas the Messenger's comments, as More reports the examination, possess the openness of a genuine response. More's stamp marks the Messenger in a way it never did his son-in-law Roper, whose burning conviction made him 'long to be pulpited', and also led him to trouble at the hands of Wolsey's administration:[21] 'The cool-hearted even slightly cynical Messenger is never likely to get himself into danger' (de Winton). In this feature, and several others we lack time to detail, he is a far call from Thomas More—the difference in voltage being precisely conducive to many sparks and occasional flashes of lightning.

Earnest game of words

It is time you should hear more than brief utterances from our London speakers of 1529. No sample of their word contest can illustrate the multitudinous matter of their debate, so I have chosen two passages that bear on its manner. You will find them in congruence with the theme of this evening—dialogue as a mode of communication congenial to Thomas More. They both occur in the middle of Book I, which takes place in More's study, with host and guest sitting at 'a little table'. The first concerns a topic that shall stay unspecified, since we want to focus on the style, in fact on a telling metaphor, which likens the dialogists to a couple of archers aiming at the same butt. It is broached by the Messenger in chapter 17:

> Sir, quod he, somewhat a little I touched it in the beginning, and made in a manner a glance thereat. But loath were I to hit with a full shot and a sharp, as I have seen some with such reasons cleave the prick in twain, that they seemed to bear over the butt and all ... (*EW*, p. 138 B)

Answers More:

> I trust that all their shots shall be so far too feeble to bear over the butt, that few of them shall touch the mark; many too faint to pierce the paper; and some too high, and some too short; and some walk too wide of the butt by a bow. (*EW*, p. 138 C)

Isn't it clever to use the bow as a unit of distance when the talk is about archery, or *toxophilia* as Roger Ascham called the game? Remember that the English were proud of their long-bow, to which they attributed their proudest victories over the French, so the bow as a yardstick is perhaps to be understood lengthwise, rather than from end to end of the bowstring [22] —see the problems besetting editors of More? Which reminds me of a sentence we encountered when sampling *Utopia*, where Peter Giles says to More, in the Yale version, 'You are quite mistaken.' The Latin behind this unpoetic banality is 'aberrasti longissime' (*CW*4, p. 48/30), literally 'Thou hast erred by a long way from [the point].' The image may be of roving over a long stretch away from one's destination, of going astray along some path. But, the author being English, although the speaker is from Antwerp, may we not fetch our clue from the protracted shooting metaphor in the *Dialogue concerning Heresies*? When there appears an Australian edition of *Utopia*, I suggest that 'aberrasti longissime' be englished as 'You have walked too wide of the butt [or: of the mark] by a bow.' [23]

More pursues the bow-and-arrow metaphor in the next chapter, but I want to hurry you to chapter 21 for another image. The tight discussion about the inerrancy of the Church has yielded a succession of corollaries, and 'the author' draws the conclusion that saint-worship, since the Church approves of it, 'is not erroneous but right'. The Messenger is prepared to surrender:

—Indeed, quod he, we be come back here with going forward, as men walk in a maze.
—Ye have not yet, quod I, lost all that labour. For, though ye have half a check in this point, yet have ye (if ye perceive it) mated me in another point, by one thing that is agreed between us now.
—What is that? quod he.
—This, quod I, that I have agreed as well as you that God hath given his church the right understanding of Scripture in as farforth as (be)- longeth to the necessity of salvation.
—In what point, quod he, hath that mated you?
—Why, quod I, see you not that? Nay then will I not tell you, but if you hear me; or if I tell you, yet shall ye not win the game thereby. For sith ye see it not yourself, it is but a blind matter.

—Let me know it yet, quod he, and I am agreed to take none advantage thereof.
   —On that bargain be it, quod I. (*EW*, p. 148 GH)

See how the little table in More's study has been, by the magic of dialogue, turned into a chessboard? The metaphor is sustained, and we are drawn into the game, nor do the Yale commentators find it much easier than the Messenger to spot the little victory More has granted him. But, whether or not, after trying hard, we do perceive it, our brains have been teased, and our attention sharpened against the next move on the chessboard. Playful in its form, the game is earnest in its final goal; the stakes, one might say, are no less than life or death of the soul. To mate, initially, meant to kill, as it still does in Spanish. But none of the players feels that he is staking his eternal salvation on each move of the joint quest, and nothing prevents that quest from being as zestful as it is vigorous.

Giles's *aberrasti longissime*, to quote it a third time, may also strike one as rather sharp. Peter Giles, like the Messenger and More, seems to have been schooled by that lover of rough and abrupt address, John Cardinal Morton. Yet he is not here testing More's nerve. More's reckoning, from the stranger's dress and appearance, that he was a *nauclerus* did not 'walk wide of the butt' after all; only, like the 'faint shots', it fell *short* of the butt. Raphael had struck Peter Giles as so unique that his seafaring identity had become as it were irrelevant: he was Ulysses and Plato, an ocean of experience and wisdom. The externals had revealed nothing rare to the beholder More, but let him hear Raphael to have the revelation of his true self: 'Speak, that I may see thee.' Hence, again, the irreplaceable virtue of oral communication.

There is a marked difference between the rather aggressive More of public life and of literature, and the gentler person he was among his own. We know of his scathing attack on Wolsey in the 1529 Parliament, and on Richard Rich at his trial. His humanist letters—to Dorp, to the Monk, to Oxford University, to Germain de Brie—were 'not untoothed',[24] any more than his polemics against Luther, Tyndale and the rest. There is some defiance too in the 'molestus haereticis' of his epitaph. Here we see the 'imperiosum Morum' admired by the dying Erasmus.[25] Whereas in 'disputations' under his roof, Roper—the man with whom in actual life More so often discussed religion—describes him as gentle and 'meek'. With 'learned men resorting to him from Oxford, Cambridge or elsewhere' he sometimes 'entered into argument, wherein few were comparable unto him'. When he perceived that some 'could not, without some inconvenience, hold out much further disputation with him, then, lest he should discomfort them ... would he by some witty device courteously break off into some other matter and give over' (Roper, p. 21–22). Evangelic meekness or mansuetude must have been buttressed by the impossibility to engage in true dialogue with academics who had been trained to dispute, not to converse, who 'took greater care to repeat than to respond',[26] who were too busy proving a thesis to catch the intonations of a human voice, who handled ideas rather than 'living men in real situations' (Young, p. xii). These disputants were the products of a system that young More and Erasmus and Vives had rebuked for thriving exclusively on the rigid parameters of formal logic[27] and ignoring the modulations of dialectics, which is 'the art of leading a genuine conversation' (H. G. Gadamer, quoted in Schaeffer, p. 14). Dialectics and dialogue have the same root; one might say that dialogue has dialectics and rhetoric for its parents. Not that More was unable to encounter the old-type logician on his own ground: for two years at Oxford he had been drilled in the arena of the syllogism. But he had graduated thence to a lifetime of common law, where no exercise was ever purely formal, where teaching was never divorced from real life, where the Readers (and More was one) were all practitioners. More's best biographer sums up the balanced training: 'His lucidity at marshalling the arguments was the result of his early schooling in dialectic and his subsequent training in the moots at Lincoln's Inn' (E. E. Reynolds, *The Field is Won*, p. 218). More's mastery owed a good deal also to his experience as barrister and judge, as Member of Parliament and diplomat, all careers that are vitally dependent on the art of persuasion and require unflagging and courteous attention to individual persons and circumstances.

One more remark about the contrast between the soft-spoken, delicate and considerate gentlemen whose thoughtful engagingness so won the hearts of kin and friend, and the tough wrestler of the campaigns for humanistic reform of the old faith: the world in which and for which More wrote or campaigned was a world of men, whereas his household was full of women and children. All of More's education and all of his professional life had taken place among men only. His Messenger too had been taught only by and with men, and now he tutored his master's sons, not his daughters. There was never a woman in More's retinue, any more than in the London Bar and Bench or in Parliament. A boy of 15, John Clement, was allowed to overhear Hythlodaeus's tale, but no woman utters a word throughout the *Utopia*. Under More's roof, womankind had more than its fair share—not only wife and daughters, but 'nurses and maids' too [28] —because it was his domestic utopia. His public, however, the England of lawyers and merchants and the schools, he realistically took as it was.

An authentic dialogue?
Is a proper faith subject to discussion? Can a strong believer talk exploratorily about his creed? More's friend St John Fisher speaks of his fellow bishops betraying the fortress of which they were the keepers, and he himself authored no dialogue. If defined dogma alone had been concerned, More too would have been only the knight defending the citadel of the faith, as he was in other polemical works, using the Bible and the Church fathers as a quarry of material to buttress the bastion that was being stormed, and as an arsenal for ammunition to fight the assaulters. But the 'diverse matters' he examined in 1529 did not all belong to the substance of the Christian revelation. Otherwise his dialogue would have pertained to

the prosperous genre of question and answer catechism.[29] He would have been exposing, at best elucidating foregone conclusions. And there is a measure of that catechetical approach in our *Dialogue*. But by far the larger part of the matter has to do with what we call 'the sciences of man': the psychology of dissent, the philology of Tyndale's *New Testament*, the history of Lutheran violence, the circumstances that led to the harsh handling of heretics, the exact tenor of the church law concerning vernacular Scripture, and so on. The Author is and plays the well-read and seasoned lawyer baring the roots of much prejudice and taking his guest to the sources, opening for him the dossier of an immemorial quarrel further complicated of late by the cross-currents of humanism and the Reformation. Plato and Aristotle have their word to say, and they say it, in the 'theologia scolastica': how much more so in this 'theologia civilior'[30] whose object is popular religion, and generally being Christian men within and not outside a Church that is by definition a mixed field of tares and good corn, which is even a ship of fools, now tossed in a tempest, yet not to be deserted simply because one cannot control the winds.[31] More's theology, to use a fashionable epithet, is pastoral. The flock for which Christ shed his blood is made of creatures of flesh and blood, to be taken as they are, to be humoured as well as fed. The irrational behaviour of the populace is harmless in comparison with the dogmatic arrogance of the old mandarins and the new self-appointed doctrinaire preachers. Nor does More adopt the stance of an arbiter passing judgement in the name of the faith or of common sense. He too is asking himself how to be a Christian in London today. As Louis Schuster writes, 'it seems probable that the oppositions which the Host and the Messenger objectify and dramatize exist as oppositions within More's sensibility' (*CW* 8, p. 1143). He borrows the eyes of his youthful partner to recapture the vision of his own youth—no angle is to be left untried in the attempt to decipher the signs of the times. More has, over the years, listened to his daughters and their husbands. He was on the Continent for a few months in 1527. His antennae are deployed and stretched to catch any voice that can further the emergence of practical truth.[32]

If the spirit of dialogue is not lacking, what about the form? The 1529 *Dialogue* has been hailed as a success by literary experts, even by C. S. Lewis, who is a half-hearted admirer of More's polemical style. Charles de Winton praises More for availing himself of 'an opportunity to pay homage to Plato in the service of the Church'. Anthologies have often selected peaks of excellence such as the dramatic sketch of Hunne's trial, framed within the broader structure. The naturalness of the tone could be questioned in places, if More claimed to be giving us a live recording, but his preface disposes of this objection. Thus he makes free use of an artifice analogous to the stage convention that allows a character to cast knowing winks or confidential information to the public over the shoulders of another *dramatis persona*. For instance, More and the Messenger, excellent Latinists both, usually translate the Latin phrases they borrow from the Vulgate; they bother to define semi-technical terms like *hyperbole* or *latria*; they make sure St Luke is known to have authored the Acts of the Apostles. Most of this is thrown in for the benefit of the audience, the *idioti homines* Tunstal has commissioned More to write for.[33] We may justify the fact by calling it a convention of the genre, but it hardly needs that justification since, in actual unedited conversation, we all say to each other a good deal that 'goes without saying'.

'This is a colloquy, it has nothing of a book about it', writes Petrarch in presenting one of his books;[34] but Castiglione makes no fuss about calling his great dialogue a book in the very title, *Il libro del Cortegiano*; and More is just as qualmless about the fact that his published *Dialogue* is a book. One major theme of it is that 'Christ left never a book behind him of his own making.' Yet it is perforce through the medium of a book that More defends the orality of the Christian revelation and denounces his age's infatuation with the written, and especially the printed, word. From the raw material of a fictional conversation, dug of course from hundreds of actual conversations, to the texture of a 'treatise', a transmutation has to take place. More does not pretend to be a notary divulging the minutes of a meeting. His preface places the final product at several removes from the 'communication had' between him and another man. He takes all of us into his authorial confidence, recounts each stage of the composition, from the rough notes made on the eve of the first session, through the manuscript duly shown to several wise experts, to the fine folio available in the shop of Master John Rastell, 'at the sign of the Mermaid'. The substantial additions in the 'overseen' text of 1531 take us one further step from the oral matrix.

For all this forging and tinkering, the craftsman felt certain that he had negotiated the hurdles of the genre and broken no rule of the game, as appears from his laughing loud, three years later, at the artistic flaws in Christopher Saint-German's anonymous dialogue of *Salem and Byzance*. Why should two Englishmen, he asks, go by such incredible names? (*EW*, p. 933 A) And 'Then stand they both still as they first meet, and that is in the street by likelyhood . . . at the least four or five hours.' (*EW*, p. 933 F) Remember that when Morus finds Giles and Hythlodaeus conversing in the marketplace, and finds further that the stranger is worth a proper hearing, his immediate movement is to take them along to his own lodging, where they all sit comfortably in secluded attention, with strict orders 'that we not be disturbed'. Another serious breach of verisimilitude in *Salem and Byzance* is where one of these fellows refers the other to 'the next chapter hereafter ensuing' (*EW*, p. 933 C), a point, says More, 'not only . . . far from the nature of a dialogue, but also from all reason'.[35] Not that there is anything wrong in the book's having chapters: More almost sports this feature in his own *Dialogue* by prefixing a table of the chapters. But these legitimate fruits of later editing are foolishly out of place on the speakers' lips. On the other hand, there is no problem with a phrase such as 'Of that point . . . I shall speak in the fourth part' (Book I), since both men mean business, and have agreed on an orderly development of their conference.

At one point, however, the vigilant and circumspect author is caught napping. After quoting a report of Luther's bragging behaviour at Worms, he adds: 'Ye that read this . . . ' (IV, 4, *EW*, p. 255 G). The simple explanation of this slip is that the passage is a close translation of a similar chapter in More's 1523 *Responsio ad Lutherum*. Whoever did the englishing—perhaps one of More's children—included the phrase: 'At nunc, obsecro, lector, vide . . . ' (*CW* 5, p. 48).[36] The Lutheran document is one of several ready-made chunks that More, working against time, incorporated into his *Dialogue*. Others are declamations à la Quintilian against Luther's denial of free-will. To break the oratorical flow of these 'inveighing' chapters with interruptions would have required no mastery, but More (as we know from the metrical licences of his Latin poems) was never a slave to his mould. He clearly chose to maintain the tightness of his discourse where the matter called for accumulation and vehemence or indignation. Book IV became the receptacle for these extraneous materials. By now the reader's mind is engaged, and the longer and shriller pieces by one voice do not mar the overall effect any more than soliloquies or tirades ruin a stage-play.[37]

1528–1529: Season of the Great Dialogues

I have already evoked the seminal role of Plato, who created dialogue as literature (and philosophy), of Cicero, who brought it from Athens to Rome, and of Lucian who popularized it and sharpened its satirical edge. By the bulk and the quality of their translations from Lucian, Erasmus and More were the main ushers of the Greek satirist into the broad stream of Latin humanism. No work of More went into so many editions in his lifetime as his *Lucianica*. His *Utopia*, though less than Erasmus's *Moria*, bears the mark of Lucian's irony, recaptures the light tone of the model.

But apart from the masterpieces of great writers, dialogue had been the vehicle of thousands of treatises. It was used in Lucian's own century by St Justin, philosopher and martyr, in defence of the Christian faith.[38] Pastors and educators were encouraged to use it by the example of St Gregory the Great, who, at the turn of the tide from Roman antiquity to mediaeval Christendom, wrote his famous *Dialogus*, a book unsurpassed in popularity through the next thousand years. Gregory deserves the more attention from us here because his prestige reached its peak in England, which he had evangelized through St Augustine of Canterbury,[39] and because he looms larger than any other Church father in More's *Dialogue concerning Heresies*.[40] Several features of the *Dialogus* may have exerted direct influence on More. The division into four books is so essential to its structure that it is mentioned in the title: *Dialogus beati Gregorii papae ejusque diaconi Petri in quattuor libros divisus*. Peter the deacon has the initiative of the conversation; he is an eager young man like More's Messenger; he puts the questions,[41] so the exchange reverses the pattern of *Erotemata* and catechisms. The longish subtitle allows a fair diversity of matter: 'de vita et miraculis patrum italicorum, et de aeternitate animarum'. The spiritual unity is ensured by the fact that the two speakers, who in age and function are like father and son, turn together toward their common ancestors, the *patres italici*, monks and hermits who in this land of theirs 'forsook this world with their whole soul'.[42] The result is a kind of breviary of otherworldliness, or of God's service. The pious anecdotes, with a heavy sprinkling of miracles, are interpreted in the light of Holy Scripture, and a number of wise rules emerge from them; the approach, then, is inductive rather than magisterial. More's wide range of topics, his way of bringing biblical precedent or teaching to bear on church history, place his *Dialogue* in the mighty wake of Gregory's.

Though there was never a dearth of dialogues, a fresh flowering of the genre can be witnessed in More's days. Times of mutation are times of probing and of querying. Hundreds of dialogue titles could be listed for the years 1525 to 1530. Let me mention three that are close to More in space or in subject-matter: Wolfgang Capito's *Brief Dialogue between a Christian father and his stubborn son*, englished by William Roy (Strasbourg, 1527) is a Reformed catechism; Juan de

Valdés's *Diálogo de doctrina cristiana* (Alcalá, 1527) is somehow its Catholic counterpart; while More's colleague, Polydore Virgil, situates in the open air near London his Three Books of Dialogues *De Prodigiis,* with Robert Ridley for his interlocutor (Basle, 1526 and subsequent editions).[43] Emerging from the tidal wave are two books for all seasons: Erasmus's *Dialogus Ciceronianus* (Basle, March 1528) and Castiglione's *Libro del Cortegiano* (Venice, April 1528), issuing from the world's noblest presses (Froben and Aldus) in the very weeks when More was invited by his bishop to enter the arena of English controversy, and when, we may presume, he set his hand to the plough. Erasmus's book may well have swayed him in the direction of dialogue. The *Convivia* and *Colloquia* published over the past ten years had made it clear that dialogue had become Erasmus's favourite medium. Together they constituted a mighty corpus, and they have stood the test of time. Yet never had Erasmus used the label *Dialogus,* which he reserved for this larger and deeper book. His theme, expressed in the subtitle 'de optimo genere dicendi', possessed burning actuality, and the work shook the Republic of Letters. This breviary of Latin style, drawing its rules inductively from a review of the day's major authors, whether living or recently dead (like Christophe de Longueil), turned out to be a definition of the Christian man of letters. The truth that inspires Buffon's dictum 'Le style, c'est l'homme' was a truism for Erasmus and his sophisticated readers. 'Speak that I may see thee' applies again. Style mirrors a whole way of thinking, living and being. Whether or not, amid the labour of forging ahead with his own project, More took time to read his friend's bomb of a book, and whether or not the *Ciceronianus* had anything to do with his own choice of a form, the parallel between the two works goes well beyond their common mould and their contemporaneity. Both are pleas for catholicity against the meagre diet of stiff-lipped precisians. The exclusive worship of Cicero, to whom his devotees reach back across fifteen centuries of living Latin as to the sole fountain of Latin unalloyed, is closely akin to the worship of Holy Writ as the only source of the Christian Revelation across fifteen centuries of living tradition. *Unus Cicero legendus*[44] and *Sola Scriptura* are twin slogans, born of the same egg. However different the objects of their jealous passion, Christophe de Longueil (Erasmus's *bête noire*) and William Tyndale (More's main butt) belong to the same sectarian family of minds. Puritanism and purism have identical roots in the human psyche. The result is something clean, no doubt, but austere, jejune, sapless, unexposed to the hazards of growth. An antiquarian spirit, a love of the safe fossil or mummy, inspires the rigid orthodoxy of avoiding any phrase not found in Cicero, and of frowning on any formula, dogma or practice not explicit in the Bible. So, as I said, there is a profound affinity between Erasmus's code of the cultured Christian, and More's idea of a Catholic Englishman, a disciple of Christ in the Church of Christ.

It was clearly superfluous for Erasmus to specify 'de optimo genere *latine* dicendi', since neither he nor his readers deemed the vernacular tongues susceptible of 'the best kind of diction'. This illusion, so total in March 1528, startles us and seems the more enormous to our hindsight because a greater book than the *Ciceronianus* was already in the Aldine press, and it was written in the Italian of Tuscany. The *Book of the Courtier*, which Baldassare Castiglione had taken many years to lick into final shape, is, like More's dialogue, and like Gregory's, divided into four books.[45] Its purpose—*disputazioni di diverse materie* (Book I, ch. 5)—tallies verbatim with More's handling of 'divers matters'. There are common features to the careers of the authors. Both were half-hearted diplomats, both were left widowers with young children, both were portrayed by great artists: Raphael's *Castiglione* is one of the Louvre's prides. Artistic analogies are not lacking between the two dialogues, even though the Italian is only narrator, and he has a greater number of speakers under the aegis of a woman, the Duchess of Urbino. But his concern, not unlike More's, is to reach a consensus through the give-and-take of a theme-centred conversation about a complex character: the idea of the man of the world, in a context of Christendom, which is taken for granted. The new butterfly, humane and urbane, will be in living continuity with the chrysalis of medieval chivalry. The *aggiornamento* that brings Plato in does not throw St Francis of Assisi out. There will be graceful dancing, but with no exclusion of manly jousting. Thus we have again a fairly broad and elastic code, blending together the new and the old, as the dialogists embrace with one love Duke Guidobaldo and his father. The authors can hardly have known of each other's books—the Lombard died before More's was published—but they both allege the same motive for having their works printed: the fear lest a mangled text appear without their sanction, from one of the manuscript copies that are going around. Last, not least, among the shared graces of the two works: *facezie* abound, and are 'canonized', as it were, by speakers who hold themselves bound to pass the salt no less freely than the viands that it is destined to season.

Physical setting of More's dialogues
In Dolet's *Dialogus Erasmianus*—published in 1534, but for which the scene is set at Padua in July 1528—More, as we have seen, is caricatured. One feature, however, is true to him, or to his dialogues. When he reaches the quiet countryside where his partner Villanovanu, after dinner, is deambulating peripatetically with a group of his students, More, arguing that he is weary from a long ride on horseback, insists that they should sit for a worthwhile exchange. So they repair to a nearby grove and 'sit together leaning against the trees'. *Consident*[46]—the word might well come straight from the *Utopia*, where it is used both for the morning and the afternoon sessions: 'in horto consedentes (*CW*, p. 50/24) and 'in eodem sedili consedimus' (p. 108/27). The prefix of togetherness and community is repeated in *confabulamur* (50/25).

More clearly agrees with Rodin's *Thinker* that one should sit for deep pondering and protracted attention. Whether in his study or 'in an arbour', he and his guest sit through the four half-days of their communication. After dinner, they walk 'shortly' into and about the garden, but that is part of their recreation. They sit down again, no doubt leaning toward one another as intently as if they were playing chess, and emulating Giles and Morus, whom Raphael found 'intentos atque auidos audiendi' (108/29). It might be illuminating to pursue the sitting metaphor in More's works. In the Nine Pageants of his youth, two of the figures—not to include Manhood 'riding upon a goodly horse'—are depicted sitting. They are the last and noblest characters: Lady Eternity, 'sitting in a chair under a sumptuous cloth of state', and then the Poet, no doubt as teacher, with a caption giving us his oracle in Latin.[47]

The chair here, like the turfy seats in the Antwerp garden of *Utopia*, is for comfort, to free the mind from attention to the body, so it can concentrate. What about the garden? All of *Utopia* takes place in one, indeed 'on the same seat', morning and afternoon. In the 1529 *Dialogue* , the alternation between More's study and 'an arbour' outdoors would be dictated by reasons of comfort, too: the mornings of England can be pretty raw even in the fair season. The arbour is a hideout, away from peeping Toms and the noises of nursery or kitchen, for the speakers to 'go forth with their matter' uninterrupted. Even when a servant comes to notify them that it is meal-time, they choose to talk on for another full hour, such are the virtues of continuity. Gardens, as we know from Genesis on, were favourite places for dialogue, and not by convention alone. In the decade of great dialogues, the Orti Oricellari, in the home of the Rucellai family, were the scene of Niccolo Machiavelli's *Arte della Guerra* and Antonio Brucioli's *Dialoghi della morale philosophia*,[48] but the two authors had actually conversed and even conspired in those gardens. Before leaving Florence, allow me, for contrast's sake, to evoke Ellis Heywood's *Il Moro* of 1556, so vibrant with admiration for More. The theme, as you remember, is true happiness, and the scene is the Chelsea garden of that paragon of happiness, Thomas More. The garden itself breathes felicity, as one guest remarks; there is the idyllic vision of beautiful

Thames gleaming between the trees in their gorgeous vernal verdancy, there is a fresh lawn studded with pretty flowers,[49] and so on. None of this pastoral feeling in any of More's dialogues!

Plato's *Symposium* and Erasmus's banquet colloquies— *Convivium poeticum, convivium senile*—blend the talking-together with eating and drinking together. This must have been the case in More's household. But a dialogue is an exercise, which More firmly separates from the refreshing of the body. 'Let us go in to dine,' says More half-way through the *Utopia* (*CW* 4, p. 108/24), and he treats us to no scrap of the table-talk. Only after dinner, and after collecting his ideas, wrapped if not rapt in silent thought—'tacitus et cogitabundus' (p. 108/30)—does Hythlodaeus resume his tale, a laborious (even) if entrancing task, so that supper time finds him in great need of a rest (244/22), presumably to consist in idle chatting as well as eating.

A Dialogue of Comfort
All these paraphernalia are proved of secondary importance by the framework of More's last and greatest dialogue. In *A Dialogue of Comfort* there are neither gardens nor shared meals. Of course young Vincent is sitting, perhaps with a modicum of comfort, as he converses with his bedridden Uncle Antony. The old sage, all passion spent, and untouched by age's souring petulance, talks hopefully about the enemies of the faith, the Turks who now occupy his beloved Hungary; he even jokes about them, and about the devil too, though that one *is* dangerous if you aren't careful to avoid his claws. Antony is no guru dispensing infallible recipes. He is tentative enough to engage in real dialogue, and his younger kinsman matures perceptibly in the course of the three books.[50] More, who held a minor role in the *Utopia*, and the main role in *A Dialogue concerning Heresies*, is absent from this work. There were obvious reasons of prudence for not speaking in his own voice while he was under heavy suspicion. The hostile scoffing engendered by his 'quod I and quod he' of 1529 may also

have prompted him to choose this distancing and depersonalizing. Of Budapest, where the talking takes place, he has no more direct experience than Shakespeare has of Elsinore, Verona or the 'still vexed Bermoothes'. He could easily, through books and diplomatic friends, have given us a few glimpses of it, but he won't distract our attention from the human problems, and these are not linked with a scenery: they are much the same under all skies.

Paradoxically, none of More's books has yielded as much biographical information, especially through the merry tales. One of these is a mini-dialogue featuring an old friend of Uncle Antony who sounds surprisingly like Thomas More of Chelsea, whom we imagine by the fireside of the Great House sometime after he had resigned the Great Seal of the Realm. My friend, says Antony, who has been conducting an anatomy of Pride, was a stranger to the 'commodity of bearing rule' (perhaps we would call it lust for power) until 'his wife taught it him':

> For when her husband . . . forsook a right worshipful room [office] she fell in hand [argument] with him . . . and asked him:
> 'What will you do, that you list [care] not to put forth yourself as other folk do? Will you sit still by the fire and make goslings in the ashes with a stick as children do? Would God I were a man, and look what I would do.'
> 'My wife', quod the husband, 'what would you do?'
> 'What? By God, go forward with the best. For, as my mother was wont to say (God have mercy on her soul!), it is ever more better to rule than to be ruled. And therefore, by God, I would not, I warrant you, be so foolish to be ruled where I might rule.'
> 'By my troth, wife', quoth her husband, 'in this I dare say you say truth, for I never found you willing to be ruled yet.' (Manley p. 225)

Don't we recognize Antony's friend? Antony himself, though he is old enough to be More's father, sounds at times like his twin. The prisoner has aged rapidly; he is often weary to the point of death—'I am dying already,' he tells Cromwell; so he can project himself into the character of a frail and sick old man. On his map of our little planet, Buda and London are not far apart, Harry the eighth of the name is first cousin to the Turk and the motleyed Thames of pied beauty mingles his waters with those of a new-found bedfellow—the blue Danube.

There is a time for everything, as all sages have said after Solomon, and as More too repeatedly said and wrote.[51] A time to stand and a time to sit. In the Spring of his second year in prison, having no doubt finished his *Dialogue*, More had become a garden haunter again. The garden this time had name Gethsemane, and he would lie prostrate uniting his agony with that of his Saviour, whose dramatic soliloquies he records in his best Latin. Now on 30 April 1535 he received, and refused, a solemn offer to sit. He himself recounts it all to Margaret:

> On Friday the last day of April in the afternoon, Mr Lieutenant came in here unto me, and shewed me that Mr Secretary [Cromwell] would speak with me. Whereupon I shifted my gown and went out with Mr Lieutenant into the gallery to him . . . And in conclusion, coming into the chamber where his Mastership sat with Mr Attorney, Mr Solicitor [Rich], Mr Bedyll and Mr Dr Tregonwell, I was offered to sit down with them, which in no wise I would. (Rogers, p. 551)

Thomas More has shifted his gown in courtesy to the king's sendees. He does not condemn or contemn these five gentlemen. But he knows no real dialogue is possible with them at this stage. A sense of honour, as well as 'the safeguard of his soul' demand that he stand, though not in defiance. The perfect gentleman, who has practice in all human postures, in kneeling too and in lying prostrate, has a perfect sense of the time, but for which he would not be a man for all seasons.

Notes

This paper elaborates the Sir Charles McDonald Lecture given by the author on 16 August 1978 in the Great Hall of the University of Sydney. The 'orality' of the address has been attenuated, and some ephemeral elements born of the occasion have been left out.

1. Roland Bainton, *'Here I Stand': a Life of Martin Luther*, New York, 1950. The words 'Hier sehe ich' did not appear in the first report of the confrontation.
   For economy of space, further references will be given in parenthesis within the text. The specific bibliography is here listed under two headings.

   More's works
   —*Works of Sir Thomas More in the English tongue*, the Rastell folio of 1557 (Scolar Reprint 1978). The siglum for these English Works in *EW*.
   —The Yale edition of More's *Complete Works* is designated by *CW* and the volume number: *Utopia* is *CW4* and *A Dialogue of Comfort* is *CW12*. As the *Dialogue concerning Heresies* has not yet been published by Yale, references to it will be by book (four books), with sometimes the chapter, or else the page in *EW*. Both *Utopia* and *A Dialogue of Comfort* are available in Yale paperbacks.
   —Elizabeth F. Rogers, *The Correspondence of Sir Thomas More*, Princeton U.P., 1947 (referred to as *Rogers*).
   —Elizabeth F. Rogers, *St Thomas More: Selected Letters*, Yale U.P., New Haven, 1961 (cited as *SL*).
   —P. S. Allen et al., *Opus Epistolarum Des Erasmi*, 12 volumes, Oxford, 1906–1952. The English edition by Toronto University Press, now under way, follows the numbering of Allen. We indicate the volume, and number of page or epistle.

   Other Works
   —David M. Bevington, 'The Dialogue in *Utopia*: Two sides of the question', in *Studies in Philology*, LVIII (1961), pp. 497–509.
   —Charles de Winton, '*The Dialogue concerning Heresies*: A neglected masterpiece', unpublished paper delivered at Thomas More Congress, Angers, April 1977.
   —Walter M. Gordon, 'Literary and Dramatic Elements in the Writings of Thomas More', unpublished Ph.D. dissertation, London University, 1966.
   —Robert F. Jones, 'On the Dialogic Impulse in the Genesis of Montaigne's *Essais*', in *Renaissance Quarterly* XXX, 2 (Summer 1977), pp. 172–80.
   —C. S. Lewis, *English Literature in the Sixteenth Century, excluding Drama*, Oxford U.P., 1954.
   —Walter J. Ong, *Ramus, Method and the Decay of Dialogue*, Cambridge, Mass., 1958.
   Walter J. Ong, 'Oral Residue in Tudor Prose Style', in *PMLA* LXXX (1965), pp. 145–154.
   —E. E. Reynolds, *The Field Is Won: The Life and Death of St Thomas More*, London and Milwaukee, 1968.
   —William Roper, *The Lyfe of Sir Thomas Moore, Knighte*, ed. E. V. Hitchcock, E.E.T.S., London, 1935. Various popular editions available.

- John D. Schaeffer, 'Dialogue and Faith in More's Humanism: Voice and Belief in the Structure of the *Dialogue concerning Tyndale*', unpublished Ph.D. dissertation, Saint Louis University, 1971.
- R. J. Schoeck, 'On Reading More's *Utopia* as Dialogue', in *Moreana* 22 (May 1969) pp. 19–32.
- Richard S. Sylvester, 'The Three Dialogues of Thomas More', unpublished paper read at Thomas More Congress, Angers, April 1977.
- C. E. Leighton Thomson, ed., *Thomas More Through Many Eyes*, London, 1978.
- Archibald Young, 'Thomas More and the Humanistic Dialogue', unpublished Ph.D. dissertation, University of Toronto, 1972.

2. 'all the way to the community of wives', adds Erasmus, in his letter of July 1519 to Hutten (Allen 2, ep. 999).
3. ibid.: 'comoediolas et scripsit et egit'.
4. '... comoediam illam quae de Salomone est' (Rogers p. 3/2). The title suggests a biblical drama.
5. Roper, in the Yale edition of Cavendish, *Life of Wolsey*, and Roper's *Life of More*, by Davis Harding and R. S. Sylvester, entitled *Two Early Tudor Lives,* New Haven, 1962, p. 198.
6. 'A mery gest how a sergeant wolde learne to playe the frere' is the first item, non-paginated, in *EW*.
7. In the paperback edition of the *Dialogue*, by Frank Manley, Yale U.P., New Haven, 1977, p. 142.
8. 'Nempe reuerso domum, cum uxore fabulandum est, garriendum cum liberis, colloquendum cum ministris, quae ego omnia inter negocia numero, quando fieri necesse est ... ' (*CW* 4, p. 38/28f.)
9. 'Mellitissima confabulatio' (*CW* 4 p. 48/14). *Fabulare* denotes very familiar talk. When, immediately thereafter, More spots Peter in conversation with a stranger, he uses the same word as of himself conferring with his domestics: 'colloquentem ... cum hospite' (48/18).
10. *CW* 13, p. 226/16: 'Gladly to be thinking of God'; 226/26–27: 'Gladly to bear my purgatory here/To be joyful of tribulations'.
11. Rogers, p. 563/57. The Latin comes on p. 561/47: 'vbi non erit opus epistolis, vbi non distinebit nos paries, vbi non arcebit a colloquio ianitor'.
12. *Essais*, III, 8: 'Conversation is, in my opinion, the most fruitful and natural exercice of our mind.'
13. This echoes, not directly Luke 10:38f., but Pico della Mirandola's letter to A. Corneo, as translated by More in his *Life of Picus*: 'I desire you not so to embrace Martha that ye should utterly forsake Mary' (*EW*, p. 14D).
14. More is here answering George Joye's anonymous *Supper of the Lord*. His *Answer* to that 'poisoned book' is awaiting a critical edition. The retort comes in Book V, ch. 1, *EW* p. 1133. More is true to his pattern: in the many dialogues within the Dialogue, 'quod he' can be someone else than the Messenger, and one encounters 'quod she', 'quod her gossip', etc.

15. The climactic sparring begins with 'inquit ille' p. 98/8 and continues for six pages to 108/25, the link-verbs occurring at 98/10, 18; 100/3; 106/3, 12, 18, 23, 25; 108/19, 24, 25. The English equivalents stretch from p. 99/9 to 109/31, with the sensible 'said I' at 109/21. More's 'quod' may have amused his own younger contemporaries as archaic. He himself, outside of this use as a link-word, normally uses 'to say'. Is it rash to suggest that Latin usage, whereby *inquit/ inquam* are restricted to the role of dialogal tags, influenced More's English? He may have sensed the etymological kinship, endorsed by Indo-European linguistics, between the Latin root *quit* and the English verb, which, besides quod/quoth, has yielded bequeath: they are historic twins.
16. A similar *caveat* applies to the enjoyment of *Utopia* in Ralph Robynson's version, which medievalists or Tudor fans may love for the wrong reason.
17. The edition best known to modern scholars was published by Eyre and Spottiswoode, London, in 1927 and again in 1931, as *A Dialogue Concerning Tyndale*.
18. I mean 'form' in the hylomorphic sense the term has in Aristotelian and Thomistic philosophy. The soul 'in-forms' the body. The spirit 'in-forms' the letter. Charity 'in-forms' faith, giving it life.
19. Which of the two Universities is More's secret, and one of his many tricks for giving his work a general application. Cambridge, Bilney's alma mater, with the 'Little Germany' of the White Horse Inn, was more touched by the new ideas.
20. *Haeresis*, from Greek αἵρεσις means choice, hence eventually sect.
21. 'It is evident that More likes the Messenger,' writes de Winton. 'He has made him what Cardinal Morton particularly valued in a man: outspoken within the bounds of politeness.' The allusion is to *Utopia, CW* 4 p. 58/24, where Morton is shown trying the mettle and composure of suitors for his favour. Cf. More's remarks to the Messenger (III, 11): 'Your words, quod I, be somewhat pugnant and sharp.' (*EW*, p. 224: *pugnant* is akin to *piquant*)
22. 'To draw the long-bow' still means 'to overstate'.
23. This would, as it were, establish a dialogue between More's dialogues.
24. 'also not untoothed', says More of Richard III at his birth (*CW* 2, p. 7/27).
25. In Etienne Dolet's *Dialogue Erasmianus* of 1535, the character Morus is bland and pliable and uncompelling. Hence Erasmus's grief at his friend's enfeebled image, at Dolet's 'making a timid speaker of imperious More: facit imperiosum Morum timide loquentem' (Allen, 11, 222).
26. My version of 'diligentius repetunt quam respondent' (*CW* 4, p. 70/ 14). Those disputants yield pat verbal echoes and utter mechanical verbal patterns, without giving an ad hoc existential response. They never truly address themselves as human, let alone Christian, beings to the matter in hand.

27. More's main indictment of late scholastic wallowing in logic comes in his letter to Dorp of 1515 (Rogers, ep. 15). In the same year, Erasmus denounces the same idle games in his Paraphrase on Psalm I: *Beatus Vir*. Vives first book, *In pseudo-dialecticos* (Paris, 1519), has an eloquent enough title.
28. From a prison letter already quoted (Rogers, p. 544/160). See More's letter of 3 September 1529 to his wife, in Rogers, p. 422. In his last letter from the Tower, two of the maids are specific objects of his care. In Holbein's family sketch, there are six women and four men.
29. Catechetical literature was not only religious. The famous *Erotemata* of the Greek teachers Chrysoloras and Guarini were manuals of grammar by question and answer. Hence the pattern in Latin grammars: 'Quot sunt orationis partes?', reply 'Octo', etc. The Dark Ages already had used the method.
30. Allusion to the 'philosophia civilior' of *CW* 4, p. 98/11.
31. Another allusion to *Utopia*, in the same intervention by Morus, p. 98/27–28.
32. Utopus is hopeful that, from the various religions co-existing in his island kingdom, 'truth will eventually emerge of its own force': *ipsa per se ueri uis emergat* (*CW* 4, p. 220/16).
33. Tunstal's letter of 7 March 1528 is reproduced in Rogers (ep. 160) and quoted copiously in the Introduction to *CW* 8 (*Confutation*), p. 1139. 'Idiotus' of course just means 'unlearned'.
34. 'Colloquium: nil de libro habet', in *De sui ipsius et multorum ignorantia*, ed. L. M. Capelli, Paris, 1906, p. 15.
35. See in *CW* 12, p. 340, the commentary on the word 'chapiter' (p. 9/17), which I feel does not quite see the point of More's strictures on *Salem and Byzance*. Surely chapters, present even in *Utopia* by way of marginal glosses, are no problem when it is understood that the 'communication' has been put on the literary anvil.
36. The two narratives (*Responsio* 1, 2 and *Dialogue* 4, 4) are sampled in *Moreana* 46 (May 1975), pp. 82–3, in parallel columns. The translator was no apprentice, as can be seen by renderings that are quite faithful though free from word-for-word slavishness, for instance 'obsecro' englished as 'for God's sake'.
37. One might add: as lecturers or media programmers announce their plan with no forfeiture of true orality.
38. Justin's *Dialogue with Trypho* was known of in More's days, but stayed unprinted until after his death.
39. The missionary band of AD 597 came from Rome to turn the Angles into angels, and Bede tells the story in his *Ecclesiastical History*. On 1 July 1535 More reminded his judges that Gregory was in a special way the father of Christian England, which doubled the impiety of England's repudiating papal authority (*Roper*, p. 94).
40. St Gregory is at the heart of a long addition to the text in the revised edition (1531).

41. It goes 'per inqisitionem et responsionem', the pope satisfying the curiosity of his deacon.
42. 'qui praesens saeculum tota mente reliquerunt' (Preface). I have used the editions of 1514 and 1516 in the Beinecke Rare Book Library, Yale University.
43. *Dialogorum de prodigiis libri tres.*
44. From Dolet's *Dialogus Erasmianus*, rep. E. V. Telle, Droz, Geneva, 1974, p. 59.
45. The Urbino conversation lasts all through the night, till dawn glows across the windows of the palace; this may hail back to the most famous chapter in Gregory's *Dialogus*, the farewell encounter between St Benedict and his sister Scholastica (a few days before her death), also a pernoctatio.
46. 1974 Reprint, p. 13.
47. *St Thomas More: The History of Richard III and a Selection from the English and Latin Poems,* ed. R. S. Sylvester, Yale University paperback, New Haven, 1976, pp. 114–18.
48. First ed., Venice, 1526.
49. *Il Moro: Ellis Heywood's Dialogue in Memory of Thomas More*, ed. Roger Lee Deakins, Harvard University Press, Cambridge, Mass., 1972, p. 14: 'Il bel Tamigi ... una continua verdura', etc.
50. Frank Manley writes (Yale paperback, p. xxxvii): 'there is throughout the final book much more true engagement and 'enterparling' of minds than we have seen in the first two books ... young and old have been truly brought together within the flexible and all-inclusive movement of the dialogue'.
51. Ecclesiastes 3:1–8. More's echoes from it are quoted in Germain Marc'hadour, *The Bible in the Works of St Thomas More*, Part I (Nieuwkoop, 1969) p. 187: 'There is, as Scripture saith, time to speak and time to keep thy tongue' (3:7).

ST THOMAS MORE AS ENGLISH POET
A. C. COUSINS

More wrote most of his English poems when he was quite young, and they imply that he knew from the start what a public life could offer him. His last poem, written in the Tower, calmly attests from experience to what he had always known possible from his days as a student. Clearly, More thought disillusion a necessary quality of an adult mind. And in his own cool dismissing of illusions there was nothing merely conventional, escapist or weak; rather, from that habit of mind he drew strength. His poems argue how precariously the impulse to order exists in society. More acknowledges that an order of the spirit may be achieved, and that eternal law takes all things into account. He stresses, however, that between these inner and transcendent orders lie the world's inescapable confusions and incongruities, and it is here that the mind's impulse to order creatively must be expressed, even though one recognizes the ultimate futility of doing so. More shows us unemotionally that order in society is at best local and momentary—won painfully and sure to be suddenly lost. A detailed understanding of all this forms an essential introduction to his major writings in prose, and persuades us of his importance as an early Tudor poet.

That determined clarity of mind in More's poems suggests the literary context from which they should be seen as emerging. The fifteenth-century lyric of moral analysis and counsel argues contempt for the world, or Boethian values, in a rhetoric assertively terse, lucid and unadorned. Its preoccupations, decisive values and refined style anticipate those of More. Both in earlier poems of that kind and in his, it is assumed that there is a hard centre of moral fact to experience —and its austerity naturally restrains the art fashioned to argue it. Here is a typical poem in this mode.

> Alas! deceite that in truste is nowe,
> Duble as Fortune, turning as a balle,

> Brotylle at assay like the roten bowe:
> Who trusteth to trust is redy for to falle.
> Suche gyle is in trust almost overalle
> That in pointe a man no frende finde shalle:
> Wherfore, beware of trust, after my devise!
> Trust to thyselfe, and lerne to be wise.[1]

Upon reading the poem, we are struck by three things. First: the mode it typifies looks back to Priscian's theory of *sententia* as a literary form, rather than just a figure of style—so that mode cannot simply be called a 'native' one.[2] Second: in its vigorous plainness, severely limited technique and direct attack on Fortune's deceits in a disordered world, the poem has affinities with the poetry of More. Third: although shrewd, the poem lacks the acuteness, the suggestive patterning, of Chaucer's 'Balade de Bon Conseil'; not until More begins to write do we find the equal of that lyric. And there is my main point. If we consider this tradition of the lyric from Chaucer onwards, we see directly that More's poetry crowns it. He sums up and extends its characteristic arguments and he re-creates its stylistic possibilities. Further, lyrics in this mode urge retreat from the world, but More, accepting the values these lyrics express, never counsels retreat. Behind his verse lies the belief that one must confront the world, and in doing so, try to order it.

A glance at More's poems on Fortune will start to make what I have been saying specific. In the prefatory poems to his 'boke of Fortune', More argues that the world is disturbed partly by Fortune, but equally by those who *refuse* to see the transience, the unreality, of her goods. He points out that although we see the result of her acts as confusion, Fortune in fact works according to laws of her own, which are hidden from men:

> ... it is fortunes guyse,
> To graunt no manne all thyng that he wyll axe,
> But as her selfe lyst order and devyse.[3]

Men, however, by their freely willed commitment to the illusions she offers them, choose to disorder their own lives, and those of others. As More says:

> Sometyme she loketh as lovely fayre and bright,
> As goodly Venus mother of Cupyde.
> She becketh and she smileth on every wight.
> But this chere fayned, may not long abide.
> There commeth a cloude, and farewell all our pryde.
> Like any serpent she beginneth to swell,
> And looketh as fierce as any fury of hell.

. . . .

> Then as a bayte she bryngeth forth her ware,
> Silver, gold, riche perle, and precious stone:
> On whiche the mased people gase and stare,
> And gape therefore, as dogges doe for the bone.
> Fortune at them laugheth, and in her trone
> Amyd her treasure and waveryng rychesse,
> Prowdly she hoveth as lady and empresse.

> Fast by her syde doth wery Labour stand,
> Pale Fere also, and Sorow all bewept,
> Disdayn and Hatred on that other hand,
> Eke restles watche fro slepe with traveayle kept,
> His eyes drowsy and lokyng as he slept.
> Before her standeth Daunger and Envy,
> Flattery, Dysceyt, Mischiefe and Tiranny.[4]

More does not write only to show that Fortune is untrustworthy—the aim that satisfied his predecessors. He wants to dismiss the illusion that men are Fortune's unwilling victims and that they are helpless before her. Quite decisively, he states that 'Eche man hath of him self the governaunce'.[5]

As these poems show, More values the wisdom of others who have confronted Fortune (especially Boethius), but he extends and clarifies their thought by arguing man's voluntary blindness in choosing to advance Fortune's power. Just as he makes his own that wisdom affirmed by a tradition of lyric opposed to Fortune and attachment to the world, so More recreates the stylistic possibilities of that tradition of verse. Here is the first stanza of 'Thomas More to them that seke fortune':

> Whoso delyteth to proven and assay,
> Of waveryng fortune the uncertayne lot,
> If that the aunswere please you not alway,
> Blame ye not me: for I commaunde you not,
> Fortune to trust, and eke full well ye wot,
> I have of her no brydle in my first,
> She renneth loose, and turneth where she lyst.

Here, as generally in More's poems, his basic unit of design is the rime-royal. More often uses the rime-royal, both as a stanza and as a distinct form; in either case he tends to make it akin to the epigram, through tactics of compression, omission and sudden counterpoint.[6] But the result is not a merely obscure style or one laconically didactic in the manner of the fifteenth-century moral lyric. As the stanza just quoted suggests, we find quite the opposite, and in fact a central characteristic of More's verse, in 'Thomas More to them that seke fortune', where the rime-royal structures a verse-epistle. More uses figures of brevity to create the tone and movement of intimate, lucid dialogue. In doing so, he creates the first real equivalent in English verse to an Attic style. We may never know whether the prefatory poems to his 'boke of Fortune' were published in his lifetime, but perhaps it is to More (rather than to Wyatt in his satires) that we should look for the model of the Attic style in English Renaissance poetry.

To make those remarks specific, I want to try to look for a moment at the first stanza of 'Thomas More to them that seke fortune' as if through the eyes of a sixteenth-century reader. Like us, a contemporary reader of the lines would have been impressed by the assurance and reasonableness of the voice speaking from the page, its confidently varied tone as it moves from one aspect of an argument to another. But the contemporary reader might also have recognized that More's sophisticated plainness, with its determination to address the reader directly and personally, has behind it a developed critical theory of persuasive argument. As a scholar in the arts of grammar and rhetoric, More must have known well Cicero's definitive account of the plain stylist as

> [though] restrained and plain, [and following] the ordinary usage, really differing more than is supposed from those who are not eloquent at all. Consequently, the audience, even if they are no speakers themselves, are sure they can speak in that fashion. For that plainness of style seems easy to imitate at first thought, but when attempted nothing is more difficult.[7]

And in confirmation of those remarks, a sixteenth-century reader might have noticed the following. First: as a whole, 'Thomas More to them that seke fortune' is carefully organized as an 'oration deliberative', so More blends an apparent ease and flexibility of discourse with the closely ordered techniques of a deliberative rhetoric.[8] For example, in the poem's first stanza, which acts as the *exordium*, it can be seen how *captatio benevolentiae* (11.1–4, though it sets the tone of the entire stanza), *anteoccupatio* (11.3–5), *apostrophe* (1.4), *testatio* (11.4–6), *experientia* and *acclamatio* (11.5–7) create a tight pattern of argument without marring the graceful informality of the speaking voice. Second: given an awareness of More's sophistication, a contemporary reader would have had a sharper understanding than we have of how More tries to use metaphoric language. According to Cicero, the plain stylist should seek to fashion tropes that are homely, clear and argumentative rather than ornamental. That aptly describes More's imagery, a striking instance occurring in the lines 'I have of her [Fortune] no brydle in my first,/She renneth loose, and turneth where she lyst'.

The image argues the impossibility of man's dominating the world's flux by the sheer disparity of its terms: the familiar object for controlling an animal is set ludicrously against the stately personification of Fortune. But the image is not comic.

On the contrary, More uses the homely, ordinary 'brydle' to suggest an infinite futility; he has a sure instinct for making us perceive the resonance of the commonplace. There are many images like that of the 'brydle' in More's Latin as in his English poems, and almost always they lead us from the familiar to the universal or eternal, and their purpose is moral argument.[9]

I have suggested that in extending the characteristic arguments of the fifteenth-century moral lyric, and in recreating its stylistic possibilities, More writes a small but highly sophisticated collection of poems that express a disillusioned clarity of moral analysis in the clarity of an Attic style. More, then, sums up a tradition of writing and does something entirely new at the same time. But there is another thing I should like to suggest about More's poems.

Again and again in his poems, More asserts or implies that one can hope to order only the inner life ('Eche man hath of him self the governaunce') as the world is beyond any definite control. Despite that, More's response is to challenge the world's disorder, not to flee it; as I suggested earlier, he would struggle to bring to society the order of the spirit, never forgetting as he does so that the effort is finally vain, for all order achieved is at best local and momentary. The first book of *Utopia* examines that idea in detail, but More had already examined the idea in his 'Pageant Verses', and I want now to look at them, closing my discussion with an account of the work that sets More's other poems in their true perspective.

The nine dramatic emblems that make up the 'Pageant Verses' take us suddenly from a study of childhood to a perception of eternity engulfing all human things. More puts human life and its concerns in the context of universal forces (like love and time) and the final timelessness that encompasses even them. He is examining human possibilities *sub specie aeternatis*, so he begins with childhood:

> I am called Chyldhod, in play is all my mynde,
> To cast a coyte, a cokstele, and a ball.

A toppe can I set, and dryve it in his kynde.
But would to god these hatefull bookes all,
Were in a fyre brent to pouder small.
Than myght I lede my lyfe alwayes in play:
Whiche lyfe god sende me to myne endyng day.

The opening words, 'I am called Chyldhod', convey the simplicity of childhood, but More will unsentimentally suggest how ambivalent that simplicity is. Childhood's conscious impulse is to thoughtless pleasure simply imagined. Unselfconsciously, however, Childhood discusses the desire to play in a syllogistic argument, and has a childish try at defining what he seems to enjoy best (1.3). In brief, we are shown from the start that man's mind has diverging impulses: one to pleasure, the other to order experience, and the impulse of pleasure itself, by reason. As the syllogistic design of the speech and the attempt at definition imply, the education that Childhood rejects (11.4–5) is being used to express Childhood's impulse to order, is becoming in fact, the basis of Childhood's way of dealing with things. So More puts forward the possibilities open to man from the beginning; then, in the emblem of Manhood, we are shown the result of following one rather than the other.

In contrast to Childhood, Manhood quite calculatedly delivers his speech as an argument; he brusquely and complacently sums up his life in an enthymeme:

Manhod I am therefore I me delyght,
To hunt and hawke, to nourishe up and fede,
The grayhounde to the course, the hawke to the flyght,
And to bestryde a good and lusty stede.

But this is hardly the speech of an adult mind. For all his insistence on argument, Manhood goes only through the motions of reasoning: the imperfect form is there without any real substance. In the end his concern is pleasure, and his pleasures are as physical and thoughtless as those of Childhood, a point Venus will make in the following emblem when she tells of Manhood's domination by physical passion. And we remember, too, from one of Erasmus's letters, how More looked down on blood sports, as do the Utopians. Here, then, we have an image of Manhood that shows the active, central years of life made trivial by an insensitivity to the mind itself and to the lives outside one's own. Manhood need not be like this, but More implies that invariably we make it so.

The figure of Old Age, however, leads us to the heart of the matter:

> Olde Age am I, with lokkes, thynne and hore,
> Of our short lyfe, the last and best part.
> Wyse and discrete: the publike wele therefore,
> I help to rule to my labour and smart,
> Therefore Cupyde withdrawe thy fyry dart,
> Chargeable matters shall of love oppresse,
> Thy childish game and ydle bysinesse.

Whether he has the *Republic* or *On Duties* in mind here, More indicates that, in seeking to bring to society the order of the disciplined spirit, the old man fulfils one of the impulses we could see in Childhood. Yet at once the old man is beaten down by Death, and the Fame that survives him falls prey to Time. Ruthless and universal forces envelop and destroy all human attempts at order or making things endure. Eternity, the last of these great forces enveloping man, says that she will bring everything 'into nought'. All our actions fall into an infinite nothingness.

But the pageant does not end with the last words of the Lady Eternity, for the final emblematic figure is that of a poet, who challenges the apparent pointlessness of our attempts to shape life coherently. The Poet affirms our transience and littleness, yet he reminds us that we, and Eternity herself, must be seen in the ultimate context of God, who gives all things meaning:

> Ergo homines, levibus jamjam diffidite rebus,
>   Nulla recessuro spes adhibenda bono,

> Qui dabit eternam nobis pro munere vitam,
>   In permansuro ponite vota deo.

> Therefore, mortals, put no confidence hereafter in trivialities, no hope in transitory advantage; offer your prayers to the everlasting God, who will grant us the gift of eternal life.[10]

The poet also tells us that the end of his art is to civilize—to create order through persuasive images of truth:

> Has fictas quemcunque juvat spectare figuras,
>   Sed mira veros quas putat arte homines,
> Ille potest veris, animum sic pascere rebus,
>   Ut pictis oculos pascit imaginibus.

> If anyone finds pleasure in looking at these pictures because he feels that, although they are products of the imagination, still they represent man truly and with remarkable skill, then he can delight his soul with the actual truth just as he feasts his eyes on its painted image.

The poet's argument is by calculation quite simple and obvious. He implies that the mind's highest use lies in trying to connect, in a hopelessly unstable world, the uncertain lives of men and the unchanging order of God. Even if no worldly order can endure, a compromise with disorder must be attempted in that way, or else we shall be isolated within creation, and the victims of the forces within it. So we see that the figure of the Poet, who is neither old and proud nor young and complacently stupid, challenges man's apparent helplessness with an argument about, and by embodying, an ideal of the truly humane and creative life. The 'Pageant Verses' end with a clear-eyed account of human limitations, a determination to make the best of them, and More's defining his responsibilities, since here he is the poet behind the emblem of the Poet.

In sketching the contexts, scope and essential unity of More's few English poems I have been trying also to suggest that he is undervalued as an early Tudor poet. In brief, I suggest that a close reading of More's poems should establish him as the only poet at the court of Henry VIII whose art could withstand the King's betrayal of Humanism.

Notes

1. From R. T. Davies, ed. and introd., *Medieval English Lyrics: A Critical Anthology* (London: 1963), p. 161.
2. See 'Fundamentals Adapted from Hermogenes', trans. Joseph M. Miller, in *Readings in Medieval Rhetoric*, eds Joseph M. Miller, Michael H. Prosser, Thomas W. Benson (Bloomington and London; 1974), pp. 56–8. On a fifteenth-century 'native' tradition of a plain style, see Yvor Winters, 'The Sixteenth-Century Lyric in England: a Critical and Historical Interpretation', in *Poetry*, LIII (1939), 258–72; LIV (1939), 35–51.
3. Reference to More's poems is from W. E. Campbell and A. W. Reed, eds, *The English Works of Sir Thomas More*, vol. 1 (London; 1931). The only exception is the 'Pageant Verses', where I follow the text in R. S. Sylvester's *The Anchor Anthology of Sixteenth-Century Verse* (Garden City, New York; 1974). Here the lines are from 'Thomas More to them that seke fortune', st. 6, lines 1–3.
4. 'Thomas More to them that trust in fortune', st. 2, 4, 5; cf. st. 3, line 2, st. 6, lines 4–7.
5. In fact he lets Fortune say it for him: 'The wordes of Fortune to the people', st. 6, line 2.
6. In his Latin epigrams, for example, More often achieves *brevitas* through *articulus, asyndeton* and *chiasmus*.
7. *Orator*, XXIII, 76ff. Quotation is from the standard Loeb translation by H. M. Hubbell. More uses the middle and high styles at times, but only as tactical exceptions to the plain style, which dominates his verse.
8. More adheres to the basic pattern of *exordium, confirmatio, confutatio, conclusio,* omitting the *narratio* and using a number of subordinate 'divisions', in which he adduces *exempla* and proposes *sententiae*.
9. Further examples would be the image of the 'dogges' gaping for 'the bone' in 'Thomas More to them that trust in fortune', st. 4, line 4, and that of fishing in the poem under discussion, st. 2, lines 4–7. In the Latin verse, there is the beautiful *'uelut instabiles uentus quatit omnis aristas'* (*'Ad contemptum huius vitae'*, line 1), and *'Sic oleo lampas deficiente perit'* (*'Vita ipsa cursvs ad mortem est'*, line 8). Reference to the Latin verse is from L. Bradner and C. A. Lynch, eds, *The Latin Epigrams of Thomas More* (Chicago; 1953), pp. 36, 38.
10. The English translation here, and below, is cited by R. S. Sylvester from Bradner and Lynch, p. 238.

THROUGH A NEEDLE'S EYE
THOMAS MORE THE WEALTHY SAINT
BRIAN BYRON

St Mark's Gospel contains the story of the young disciple of Jesus who, while clad only in a linen cloth, witnessed the arrest of his master. When he attempted to flee like the others, the soldiers grabbed hold of the cloth. He left it in their hands and fled naked.[1]

Streakers being a fairly common sight in recent times, modern commentators usually pass quickly over this incident perhaps with only brief speculation concerning the identity of the agile disciple. Thomas More, however, was able to find a good deal to reflect upon. In his last major work, *De Tristitia Christi*, a meditation on the agony in the garden, he gives an interesting figurative interpretation of the event. I quote from Clarence Miller's beautiful translation in the recent Yale edition:

> this young man suddenly threw off the cloth . . . and fled . . . naked. . . . What is the figurative meaning of this? What else but this: just as a pot-bellied man, slowed down by his fat paunch, or a man who goes around wearing a heavy load of clothes is hardly in a condition to run fast, so too the man who is hemmed in by a belt full of money-bags is hardly able to escape when troubles descend on him and put him in a bind. Neither will a man run very fast or very far if his clothing, however light it may be, is so tightly laced and knotted that he cannot breathe freely. For a man who is wearing a lot of clothing but can get rid of it quickly will find it easier to escape than a man who is wearing only a little but has it tied around his neck so tightly that he has to carry it with him wherever he runs. One sees rich men—less often, it is true, than I would like—but still, thank God, one sometimes sees exceedingly rich men who would rather lose everything they have than keep anything at all by offending God through sin . . . On the other hand we see people—and far more of them than I would wish—who happen to have only light garments . . . and yet have so welded their affections to those poor riches of theirs that you could sooner strip skin from flesh than separate them from their goods.[2]

In brief, More's thesis in this passage is that one man may be less attached to great wealth than another is to less. The spiritual warning of More's commentary on the unencumbered young man is to keep oneself fundamentally free from riches so as to be able to escape from sin.

The object of my paper will be to explore further the manner in which More, a wealthy man, came to terms with the Gospel message regarding the abandonment of wealth. The question is still very pertinent to many Christians. Conscientious believers enjoy the benefits of the affluent society. Not only men of business, but academics and those in public life are recipients of high incomes. Indeed, the standard ambitions of many Christians lead them inevitably to a stable family life and what it requires, a sound economic position. The Church encourages thrift, the development of one's skills, the pursuit of learning and higher qualifications, the betterment of one's position, the avoidance of dead-end jobs, frugality, self-discipline, responsibility in the use of wealth, and so on. Some of the counterbalancing factors that tended to impoverish many Christians have either disappeared or diminished: the large family, the absence of state aid for church schools, discrimination in jobs on the grounds of religion. As a result, today a Christian can be financially quite well off. Such a person may find some Gospel passages rather disconcerting. Indeed they present a challenge now as they did to Thomas More. He commented on them in his writings and his ideas are well worth our attention.

There is no need to go over the well-known Gospel texts on the spiritual dangers of wealth, and in any case they will come up for comment as we proceed. But they add up to quite a formidable challenge to us today, perhaps more than ever. Besides the greater disparity in wealth, there is also more awareness of poverty in our own country as well as in the 'third world', due to the efficiency of the mass media.

Spiritual theology suggests that we look at both the theory and the practice put before us by the saints, that is, their writings and their lives. Canonization is the Church's attestation of a saint's heroic degree of virtue and his or her worthiness to serve as a model to the faithful. The Church requires proof of such virtue and she accepts martyrdom as persuasive evidence. The question is sometimes asked whether More would have been canonized had he not been martyred. Would he rate as a saint, for example, on the score of evangelical poverty?

Professor G. R. Elton has given an account of More's accumulation of lands and money as a result of his career in high public office.[3] The pursuit of wealth was not, according to Elton, a driving force in More's life, but neither did he ignore his entitlement to remuneration, and sometimes he actively sought out money that was owed to him by those who were well off.

Usually we find that saints have nothing and spend much time soliciting alms for charitable projects. In this respect More was solicited rather than a solicitor, he gave rather than collected. But then, he had enough to give. How did he justify his position?

In his writings More frequently deals with the problems of both wealth and enforced poverty. Poverty, to which many are subjected by an unjust social system, is certainly no virtue, and it brings in its train many other evils. More makes this point strongly in *Utopia*. Poverty in England, he wrote, only leads to an increase in theft.[4] By contrast, the Utopians practise economic egalitarianism so that none is poor. Moreover, they despise show and grandeur: from gold and silver they make chamber pots, and chains and fetters for slaves![5]

More touches upon the subject of the Christian's attitude to wealth in some of his controversial works. In the *Apology* he defends the majority of clergy and religious against the charge of avarice, and warns the laity that greed may be the motive of their criticism of the 'spirituality'.[6] In the *Supplication of Souls* he warns of the transience of worldly goods, illustrating his point with a picturesque description of souls in hell being tormented with a vision of their old riches, which they now see to be worthless.[7]

While More dealt with the attitude to wealth in his humanistic and controversial writings, it is in his spiritual works that we will find his most thorough treatment of the subject, and notably in the *Dialogue of Comfort Against Tribulation*.[8] This work is a conversation between Antony and his nephew Vincent, two imaginary characters, who discuss the anticipated persecution of Hungarian Christians by the invading Turks, but obviously it is meant to be more than that. The principles applied in the *Dialogue* can be applied to any Christian under threat—again obviously to More himself as he awaited the wrath of Henry VIII. In this book More argues to convince us that it is worth while enduring all persecution for the winning of Christ. This may involve the loss of the goods of fortune—lands and possessions, riches, fame, offices and authority. We will focus our attention on More's comments concerning wealth rather than the other goods of fortune, though there is a consistency in his treatment of all of them. He treats of various aspects of the question of wealth, and in one section deals directly and at length with the central problem that is worrying us: how can a Christian justify the possession of wealth when he is conscious of critical poverty around him? But let us start at the beginning.

Early in the book More displays a rather medieval attitude to worldly goods. He writes:

> Now because this world is as I tell you, not our eternal dwelling but our little-while wandering, God would that we should in such wise use it, as folk that were weary of it and that we should in this vale of labour, toil, tears and misery not look for rest and ease, game, pleasure, wealth, and felicity . . .[9]

More considers a man to be in a dangerous situation if everything is going too smoothly for him in this life. He renders the Scripture: 'Woe may you be that laugh now, for you shall wail and weep'; 'There is time of weeping, and a time of laughter'; 'They went forth sowing their seeds weeping . . . they shall come again more than laughing with great joy and exultation with their handfuls of corn in their hands'.[10] The danger of the goods of fortune to one's eternal salvation can be offset only by the endurance of a degree of tribulation. Our Lord's life illustrates the point:

> And for to prove that this life is no laughing time but rather the time of weeping we find that our Saviour himself wept twice or thrice but never find we that he laughed as much as once. I will not swear that he never did but at least wise he left us no samples of it.[11]

Scripture also bears out, says Antony, with many quotations to prove it, that God chastises those He loves, and lays a cross of tribulation upon their back.

Against this view, Vincent makes the objection that it would be strange if God were to send tribulation to those He loves as a sign of His favour, and prosperity to sinners as a sign of eternal damnation. Solomon, Job and Abraham, he points out, were virtuous people who enjoyed prosperity. Antony agrees that there is no general rule by which the good receive only tribulation and the sinner only prosperity. His contention is rather that 'continual wealth in this world without any tribulation [is] a fearful sign of God's indignation'.[12]

Solomon was not a very good example for Vincent to put forward. Though God in His love lavished wealth on him, the outcome of his life was not so edifying. As Antony observes, 'Surely we see that his continual wealth, made him fall first into such wanton folly, in multiplying wives to a horrible number . . . and taking to wife . . . such as were infidels'.[13]

Job's prosperity was interrupted by a period in which he was sorely tried, so his case only serves to illustrate Antony's point. Abraham also experienced probation—for example, in being commanded to sacrifice his son Isaac. He thereby became 'a special patriarch of the faith' and merited more by his faith and tribulation than did the poor man Lazarus. On the other hand there was another rich man well below Lazarus 'crying and calling out of his fiery couch', asking that Lazarus might put a drop of water on his burning tongue. Abraham's final words to Dives prove Antony's thesis: 'Son, remember that thou hast in . . . life received wealth, and Lazare in likewise pain but now receiveth he comfort . . . while you receive sorrow, pain and torment.'[14] Dives's problem was that he had enjoyed continuous prosperity with no tribulation. He had been guilty of 'no great heinous crime but the taking of his own continual ease and pleasure, without any tribulation or grief. Whereof grew slothe and negligence to think upon the poor man's pain.'

Temptations arising from wealth can be either subtle or overt. The first come under More's heading of the *negotium perambulans in tenebris*, the business walking in the dark, while the second he describes as the noonday devil. The *Dialogue* deals first with the subtle temptations, with a warning against covetousness. More renders St Paul: 'They that long to be rich do fall into temptation and into the grynne [snare] of the devil and into many desires unprofitable and harmful which drown men into death and destruction.'[15] The point is illustrated from the Gospel: 'The covetous man also that our saviour speaketh of in the gospel that had so great plenty of corn that his barns would not receive it but intended to make his barns larger and said unto himself that he would make merry many days had thought that he had a great way yet to walk but God said unto him, Stulte . . . Fool, this night shall they take thy soul from thee and then all this good that thou hast gathered, whose shall it be?'[16]

Then the discussion turns to the case of those 'very good folk' who find riches coming to them easily and are confronted with such words of Scripture as 'facilius est camelum per foramen acus transire quam divitem intrare in regnum Dei', which More translates: 'It is more easy for a camel or as some say (for camelus so signifieth in the Greek tongue) for a great cable rope to go through a needle's eye than for a rich man to enter into the kingdom of God.'[17]

To set good people at ease Antony gives this counsel: 'in all those places of Scripture, the having of the worldly goods is not the thing that is rebuked and threatened but the affection that the haver unlawfully beareth thereto'. St Paul's words, 'Qui volunt divites fieri', reproach not 'the having' but 'the will and the desire and affection to have and the longing for it . . . and to declare that the having of riches is not forbidden but the inordinate affection of the mind sore set thereupon, the prophet saith: "Divitiae si affluant nolite cor apponere/If riches flow unto you, set not your heart thereupon. And albeit that our Lord by the said ensample of the camel or the cable rope to come through the needle's eye said that it is not only hard but also impossible for a rich man to enter into the kingdom of heaven: yet he declared that though the rich man cannot get into heaven of himself yet God he said can get him in well enough. For unto God (he said) all things are possible.' The warning of Jesus was directed to those who put their trust in money: 'Filioli quam difficile est confidentes in pecuniis regnum dei introire: my babies how hard it is for them that put their trust and confidence in their money, to enter into the kingdom of God.'[18]

Satisfied on this point, Vincent goes on to a question that still bothers many people today: how can anyone justify the keeping of wealth when there are so many poor people in the world? He quotes St Ambrose, who said that if someone dies from poverty when we could have helped them, we are responsible for their death, 'we kill them'.[19]

Antony concedes that a rich man who keeps all his riches to himself despite poverty abounding around him should indeed fear eternal damnation. But the real question is whether a rich man must give away the greater part of his riches until he is no longer rich. It is true that Jesus did invite some men to give up everything to follow him, 'that they may the more speedily get and attain the state of spiritual perfection'. Yet he did not command every man to do so 'upon the peril of damnation'. The saying of Jesus, 'he that forsake not all that ever he hath, cannot be my disciple', is to be interpreted as hyperbole and as meaning a preference for Christ over all possessions. This is indicated by other sayings of Jesus, such as that in the preceding context in the Gospel where he said, 'He that cometh to me, and hateth not his father and mother, and his wife and his children, and his brethren and his sisters, yea and his own life too, cannot be my disciple.' In all of these sayings Jesus was teaching us to love God above all other persons and things, not literally to hate them or to abandon them. In particular, says Antony, there is no commandment forbidding a man to 'be rich or have substance'.[20]

Through Antony, More gives an interpretation of a strange saying of Jesus that follows the parable of the unjust steward who bought himself friends by writing off his master's debts (Luke 16:1–9). 'Make you friends of the wicked riches that when you fail here, they may receive you into the everlasting tabernacles.' This means, according to the interpretation given here by Antony, that the rich should use their wealth to make friends with those who practise voluntary poverty, whose intercession will then avail them in the next life. Being high in heaven because of their voluntary poverty, they will be in a position to put in a good word for their wealthy friends.[21]

Pursuing the subject, Antony says that rich men, 'to whom God giveth substance and the mind to dispose it well, and yet not the mind to give it all away at once but for good causes to keep some substance still, should not despair of God's favour', since they have received no commandment from God or any special calling to give up all. This point is supported from the Gospel by the case of Zacchaeus whom Jesus called down from the tree. Touched by grace, Zacchaeus immediately pledged half his goods to the poor and guaranteed that he would recompense fourfold any person whom he may have defrauded. The fact that he could give away half his goods and still have enough to make restitution proves that Zacchaeus did not intend to leave himself a beggar. And yet Jesus asserted: 'this day is health [More's rendering of the Latin *salus*, salvation] come to this house, for that he too, is the son of Abraham'.[22]

Despite this answer, Vincent bores in: can a rich man retain even part of his wealth while there are people in dire poverty?

This is a circumstance that is always true, rejoins Antony. As our Lord said, 'poor men shall you always have with you'. Hence there would never be anyone who would be wealthy without danger of eternal damnation. Then if there were no good wealthy people, there would be no-one to relieve the poor. Again, if all wealth were equally distributed between everyone in the country, the last state would be worse than the first, because everyone would be almost beggars.[23]

This passage could be utilized in any discussion of More's attitude to socialism. The paragraph that follows shows that for More human existence requires ownership and management of productive property by a few for the employment and benefit of many. As Antony states, 'For surely the rich man's substance is the wellspring of the poor man's living'. Aesop's fable of the hen that laid the golden eggs (hen being More's word) illustrates the need for capital possessions.[24]

Another Gospel text is now brought into the discussion: 'Give to everyone who asks'. A rich man is bound, says Antony, to give to all needy people who are 'specially by God's commandment committed unto his charge alone'. But does this mean that a rich man must give to *everyone* who asks as *much* as he asks? The rich man would soon be left with nothing. However, the context suggests that when he said, 'Give to *everyone*', Jesus was suggesting that we should come to the aid of all kinds of people, friend or foe, kin or stranger, Christian or heathen. Nevertheless, we are not bound to give the same aid to everyone. Scripture indicates a priority to those who are our own, our family and household.[25] I suppose we would now quote 'charity begins at home'. Hence we are required specially to care for our relatives and employees. We recall at this point More's solicitude for his neighbours and farmhands whose livelihoods were threatened after fire destroyed barns and corn on his property at Chelsea. Though the fire was the fault of another, More instructed his wife Alice by letter to compensate his neighbours: 'For even if I should not leave myself a spoon, there shall no poor neighbour of mine bear no loss by any chance happened in my house'.

Moreover, none of his employees was to be dismissed until further employment was found for them.[26]

But to return to the *Dialogue of Comfort*, Antony also sees a special obligation on us to care for those providentially in our keep. If servants get sick we are bound to provide for their need. And even if we happen to receive into our house a wayfarer who gets sick and runs out of money (one thinks of Erasmus) we should not thrust him out. 'For when God hath by such chance sent him to me, and there once matched me with him I reckon myself surely charged with him, till I may without peril of his life be well and conveniently discharged of him'.[27]

Hence we are bound to use our wealth to aid those in need who ask for help, no matter who they are, though there may be certain priorities in our giving. But apart from 'the case of such extreme needs well perceived and known to myself I am not bound to give every beggar that will ask nor to believe every faytour [cheat, impostor] that I meet in the street that will say himself that he is very sick nor to reckon all the poor folk committed by God to my charge alone.' I can assume that others are good enough to share the burden of alms-giving. Some people could take this line of thought to an extreme and think so highly of the generosity of others that they would leave all relief of the poor to them: 'Those are they that are content to give nought because they be nought.'[28]

It is not with such people that we are concerned. Rather, our interest is with those who are trying to dispose of wealth according to God's will. At this point of the *Dialogue* Antony gives what must be a statement of More's own policy, so I will quote it at length:

> if there be a man . . . that hath unto riches no love but having it fall abundantly unto him, taketh to his own part no great pleasure thereof but as though he had it not, keepeth himself in like abstinence and penance privily, as he would do in case he had it not, and in such things as he doth openly, bestow somewhat more liberally upon him-

self in his house after some manner of the world lest he should give other folk occasion to marvel and muse and talk of his manner and misreport him for a hypocrite therein—between God and him doth truly protest and testify as did the good queen Esther, that he doth it not for any desire thereof in the satisfying of his own pleasure but would as with good will or better forbear the possession of riches, saving for the commodity that other men have by his possessing thereof as percase in keeping a good household in good Christian order and fashion and in setting other folk awork with such things as they gain their living the better by his means: this man's having of riches I might me thinketh in merit match in a manner with another man's forsaking of all . . .'[29]

We know from More's biographers that this passage describes More's own life-style.

The discourse now turns to the temptation called the 'noonday devil', that is, open persecution. This happens when one is threatened with the confiscation of worldly possessions if he does not yield on principle. Antony sets out to demonstrate the fickleness of worldly values, the transience of reputation and power. Outward goods do little for the body and much harm to the soul. The persecution by the Turks will separate those who are concerned only for their own worldly pleasure from those who use worldly goods for virtuous purposes. These latter will be prepared to forsake worldly goods rather than deny their faith. Under open persecution there can be no compromise: 'Nemo potest duobus dominis servire: no man may serve two lords at once.'[30]

In the face of persecution, then, there is only one thing to do: 'Hoard up your treasures in heaven, where neither the rust and the moth fret them out and where thieves dig them not out and steal them away, for whereas is thy treasure there is thine heart too.'[31]

As regards temporal substance, when persecution threatens, the best thing to do is to give it to the poor:

> If we put it into the poor man's bosom, there shall it be safe. For who would go search a begger's bag for money; if we deliver it to the

poor for Christ's sake, we deliver it unto Christ himself. And then what persecutor can there be so strong, as to take it out of his hand?[32]

Further motivation to bear the loss of goods for Christ's sake is provided by the remembrance of the poverty of Jesus himself. Being universal King he gave up everything for us, even before we were his poor sinful servants, yes, when we were as yet 'his adversaries and his enemies'. Should we not then be prepared to give up everything for him when this is required? If we accept this attitude, God will 'compass us about with a pavice' (a shield) so that we need not fear the 'noonday devil'. For the loss of worldly goods 'we shall be with heavenly substance everlastingly recompensed of God in joyful bliss and glory'.[33]

The rest of the *Dialogue of Comfort* need not now concern us. Before leaving it, however, I would like to pay tribute to it as a great spiritual classic that touches very realistically on points of concern for the Christian trying to live according to the Gospel in the world. It is a book to which spiritual theologians ought to give much more attention than they do. It is available in readable editions, even in paperback, so that it is now much more accessible than ever.

We saw earlier that wealth came effortlessly to More. But he not only acquired money—he spent it. His spending was no doubt very discriminating. He did not waste money but bought well. He purchased good books, he encouraged good artists, he paid for the education of his family and wards. He furnished his house well and adorned it with interesting things. He entertained and corresponded with the best of the intelligentsia, headed by no less than the great Erasmus. He had musical instruments, which he and his wife attempted to master. His library contained the works of major writers, the Fathers of the Church, the Erasmian editions of Scripture and patristic commentaries, as well as the great theologians and philosophers.

In the normal sense of the word, however, More was not self-indulgent. His spending was on useful things rather than on items of luxury. Monetary self-interest was certainly not part of his character.

There are several interesting incidents recorded by Roper that throw a curious light on More's attitude to wealth. When he was commissioned to write against the heretics, the bishops in convocation, knowing that his polemical activities had put him under economic strain, agreed to give him a gift of four or five thousand pounds—an enormous sum in those days. When the gift was offered to him he refused it, though the bishops pressed him hard to accept. Even when they tried to persuade him to accept it for his family he declined it, saying: 'I had liefer see it all cast into the Thames than I, or any of mine, should have thereof the worth of one penny.'[34]

There is another passage in Roper's *Life of More* that shows how More adapted his life-style to his fall from favour and wealth. He prepared his family for the lower living standard by describing how he had in early life ascended gradually from the austere fare of Oxford to the only slightly better conditions of New Inn, then to the higher standard of Lincoln's Inn. To soften the blow for his family he proposed that they should not descend immediately to Oxford fare but that they should first try that of Lincoln's Inn, and if they could not afford it, they would then try New Inn's fare, and Oxford's only as a last resort. And if that became impossible, 'then may we yet with bags and wallets, go a-begging together, and hoping that for pity some good folk will give us their charity, at every man's door to sing Salve Regina, and so still keep company and be merry together.'[35]

More's refusal of the bishops' payment for his services in refuting heretics contrasts strangely with another, rather surprising and amusing, event, also narrated by Roper. It occurred on the occasion of the coronation of Queen Anne. The Bishops of Durham, Bath and Winchester requested him 'both to keep them company from the Tower to the coronation, and also to take twenty pounds ... to buy him a gown with'. More took the twenty pounds, but stayed at home! He realized that his presence at Queen Anne's coronation would be interpreted as consent to the divorce. Next time he met the bishops he explained that he felt he could more boldly deny them one request, the invitation to accompany them to the coronation, if he granted them the other, that is, the acceptance of the twenty pounds.[36]

When the heavy hand of the law confiscated More's property, and he was left virtually penniless in the Tower, his wife Dame Alice unwittingly gave testimony to the extent of More's willingness to forfeit everything for conscience' sake. Again we are indebted to Roper's account:

> 'What the good year, Master More', quoth she, 'I marvel that you, that have been always hitherto taken for so wise a man, will now so play the fool to lie here in this close, filthy prison, and be content thus to be shut up amongst mice and rats, when you might be abroad at your liberty, and with the favour and good will both of the King and his Council, if you would but do as all the Bishops and best learned of this Realm have done. And seeing you have at Chelsea a right fair house, your library, your books, your gallery, your garden, your orchard and all other necessaries so handsome about you, where you might in the company of me your wife, your children and household be merry, I must ask what a God's name you mean here still thus fondly to tarry.'
>
> After he had a while quietly heard her, with a cheerful countenance he said unto her, 'I pray thee, good Mistress Alice, tell me one thing.'
>
> 'What is that?' quoth she.
>
> 'Is not this house', quoth he, 'as nigh heaven as my own?'[37]

Another well-known story is that of the gilt cup allegedly given by a litigant to More when he was judge. Robert Bolt used the incident in his play, though with a considerable degree of dramatic licence. The tale is one of three narrated by Roper to illustrate how More's enemies accused him of accepting bribes, but of course in each instance he is completely exonerated.[38] His innocence of all charges of corruption again demonstrates how little he coveted money.

There have been many comments on More's practice and

theory of evangelical poverty. His generosity to the poor was proverbial in Shakespeare's day: the Elizabethan *Play of Sir Thomas More*, in which the great bard had a hand, describes More as 'the best friend that the poor e'er had'. Most recently the introduction to the new Yale edition of the *Dialogue of Comfort* describes More's policy on wealth. The editors detect in More's attitude to worldly possessions the Augustinian distinction between *uti* and *frui*, the use of things as contrasted with their enjoyment.[39] Certainly, More acquired things for their utility and not for mere show. One is reminded of the Utopians, who held gold and silver in contempt in comparison with the useful metal, iron. Nevertheless, I think More enjoyed some of the things that money could buy, for example, his books, his pet monkey and his fool.

Perhaps the most discerning analysis of More's regard for wealth is provided by Hans Kung. Kung, the most controversial of contemporary Catholic theologians, is at his best when describing gospel spirituality. Kung concludes his discussion of this aspect of More's character: 'the *great* test of a Christian's freedom arises when he is faced with the choice of abandoning not just something but *everything* for the sake of God and his kingdom: of giving away "all that he has" to possess the field with the hidden treasure, the pearl of great price'. This was verified in the case of More, says Kung, when he put into practice 'that radical readiness in faith which he had maintained, in principle, through all his years as a student, lawyer, judge, diplomat, and Lord Chancellor; readiness for anything, for any sacrifice . . . He renounces his possessions; he loses his income . . . submits to the confiscation of his goods. Poor, prematurely aged, and ill, leaning on a stick, the ex-lord Chancellor faces his judges.'[40]

Thomas More was indeed a man of considerable wealth for most of his life, yet by God's grace, which he would be the first to give the credit to, he got through the 'needle's eye' into the Kingdom of heaven. While he possessed wealth, he used it wisely, enjoyed what it could buy, shared it magnanimously with others, his family, friends, employees and the poor. He was ready to part with it all rather than let it stand between God and himself. This is what he prayed for as a prisoner in the Tower, in 1534:

> Give me thy grace good Lord ...
> of worldly substance ...
> to set the loss at right nought
> for the winning of Christ.[41]

Notes

1. Mark 14:52
2. *Complete Works of St Thomas More*, Yale University Press (hereafter CW), vol. 14, pp. 597–603.
3. 'Thomas More, Councillor', in *St Thomas More: Actions and Contemplation*, ed. R. S. Sylvester, Yale University Press, 1972, pp. 87–122.
4. CW, vol. 4, p. 61.
5. ibid., p. 153.
6. *The Apologye of Syr Thomas More, Knight*, ed. A. Taft, London 1930, p. 116.
7. *Workes* (1557), p. 336.
8. CW, vol. 12.
9. ibid., p. 41.
10. ibid., p. 42.
11. ibid., p. 42.
12. ibid., p. 49.
13. ibid., p. 53.
14. ibid., p. 55.
15. ibid., p. 168.
16. ibid., p. 168.
17. ibid., pp. 170–1.
18. ibid., p. 171.
19. ibid., p. 172.
20. ibid., p. 175.
21. ibid., p. 175.
22. ibid., p. 179.
23. ibid., p. 179–80.
24. ibid., pp. 180–1.
25. ibid., p. 182.
26. *St Thomas More: Selected Letters*, ed. E. Rogers, Yale University Press, 1961, pp. 170–1.
27. CW, vol. 12, 182–3.
28. ibid., pp. 183–4.
29. ibid., pp. 184–5.
30. ibid., p. 231.

31. ibid., p. 239.
32. ibid., p. 240.
33. ibid., p. 244.
34. *Roper & Harpsfield: Lives of Saint Thomas More*, Everyman's Library, 19, p. 24.
35. ibid., pp. 26–7.
36. ibid., p. 29.
37. ibid., pp. 40–1.
38. ibid., pp. 30–2.
39. CW, vol. 12, cviii.
40. Hans Kung, *Freedom in the World: St Thomas More*, Sheed & Ward, 1965, pp. 32–7.
41. CW, vol. 13, pp. 226–7.

THOMAS MORE'S USE OF SCRIPTURE IN THE DIALOGUE CONCERNING HERESIES
DENIS P. MINNS O.P.

In 1528 the Bishop of London sent Thomas More a bundle of English pamphlets published by some followers of Luther, together with some of Luther's own works. In the accompanying letter he asked More to publish 'something in English which will reveal to simple and uneducated men the crafty wickedness of the heretics, and will better equip such folk against such impious supplanters of the Church'.[1] Cuthbert Tunstall liked suggesting such tasks to his friends. When he first encountered Lutheranism in Germany in the first years of the decade, he wrote to Erasmus suggesting that he take up the fight.[2] Even so, it seems an odd task for a bishop to give a layman, and a busy senior servant of the Crown. Much later, an enforced vacation from affairs of state enabled Tunstall himself to try his hand at polemical theology. It is interesting to note that the two works he produced then were written in Latin.[3] Yet Tunstall recognized the necessity of replying to the Reformers in English, and in his letter to More he cites More's mastery of English as one of the accomplishments eminently suiting him to the proposed task. Another qualification mentioned by Tunstall was More's learning. Tunstall was himself a humanist, and familiar with Greek and Hebrew.[4] More had long since dissociated himself from the reactionary Catholic attack on Erasmus's program of biblical theology.[5] Since the status and interpretation of Scripture was bound to be a principal point at issue in any controversy with the Reformers, one wonders what expectations Tunstall had of the way More would handle Scripture.

More met Tunstall's request with the *Dyaloge of Syr Thomas More knyghte: one of the counsayll of oure souerayne lorde the kyng & chauncellour of hys duchy of Lancaster. Wherin be treated dyuers maters as of the veneration & Worshyp of ymagys & relyques prayng to sayntys & going on pylgrymage. Wyth many othere thyngys touchyng the pesty-*

lent sect of Luther and Tyndale by the tone bygone in Saxony and by the tother laboryd to be brought in to England,[6] published in 1529. In this paper I propose to ask how More approaches the Scriptures in this work, particularly with regard to the influence of the Erasmian program. I shall not consider here the second stage of the controversy—*The Confutation of Tyndale's Answer*—or any of More's other polemical works.

I

I shall consider first what More says explicitly in the *Dialogue* of the value and function of Scripture. Obviously, the *Dialogue* cannot be expected to yield a full statement of More's views on this matter. He was commissioned to write for 'simple and uneducated men'. The *Dialogue* explicitly seeks to fulfil this commission. More acknowledges that he is not an expert in the subjects he discusses,[7] and the *Dialogue* asserts itself as a work written by a layman for laymen.[8] However, this circumstance does not remove the controversy from the context of biblical humanism. Both More and the Messenger make statements about the value of Scripture that have much in common with the views Erasmus expressed in his prefaces to the various editions of his *New Testament*. Both lay emphasis on the moral and devotional value of reading Scripture. Thus the Messenger asserts that 'the scripture is to good folk the nourisher of virtue; and to them that be nought it is the means of amendment',[9] and More, that 'there is no treatise of scripture so hard but that a good virtuous man, or woman either, shall somewhat find therein that shall delight and increase their devotion'.[10] For Erasmus, this was the first and only goal of the study of Scripture: 'ut muteris, ut rapiaris, ut affleris, ut transformeris in ea quae discis'.[11] The Messenger further sees Scripture as an easily accessible font of all necessary doctrines.[12] More disagrees with this. He attributes the widest range of functions to Scripture: 'it is so marvellously tempered, that a mouse may wade therein, and an elephant be drowned therein'.[13] He does not discountenance the use of Scripture in theological argument,[14] but in his view this is not the province of the laity. For them, Scripture should be rather 'occasion of devotion than of discussion'.[15] However, since the Reformers will allow the laity to read Scripture for the purpose of ascertaining or verifying doctrine,[16] More is obliged to debate the correct way to approach the reading of it. In this he shows himself more Erasmian than the Messenger, though he changes the emphasis of the Erasmian program significantly. The Messenger's distaste for logic and reason may derive partly from the contempt for scholasticism shared by Erasmus and Reformers alike.[17] But he has no knowledge of biblical languages and considers neither the liberal arts nor the commentaries of the Fathers to be of any use in interpreting Scripture.[18] This is quite contrary to Erasmus's program.[19] In only one matter —the collation of texts for the interpretation of difficult passages—does the Messenger follow Erasmus.[20] More's rules for the interpretation of Scripture, on the other hand, can be matched point by point in Erasmus. He considers the liberal sciences to be 'handmaids to give attendance upon divinity'.[21] He advises the student of Scripture to 'study for the virtuous framing of his own affections',[22] 'to have a special regard to the writings and comments of old holy fathers',[23] and to be 'well and surely instructed in all such articles and points as the Church believeth'.[24] If the text remains obscure, he should then collate other texts, check translation, transcription and printing for errors, and if it still remains clouded, 'let him reverently knowledge his ignorance, lean and cleave to the faith of the Church as to an undoubted truth, leaving that text to be better perceived when it shall please our Lord with his light to reveal and disclose it'.[25] Even in this last point he is in accord with Erasmus, who wrote in the *Ratio Verae Theologiae:* 'quod datur videre, pronus exosculare: quod non datur, tamen opertum, quidquid est, adora simplici fide, proculque venerare'.[26]

The most significant difference of emphasis between Erasmus and More in the method of interpreting Scripture is the importance given to the rule of faith. By this rule, says Erasmus, the sense given to obscure words should be in accord with the whole body of Christian doctrine.[27] Erasmus tucks this rule away in the middle of the *Ratio* and gives it no further comment. For More, it must be the starting point of all scriptural study.[28] This derives from the conviction that Scripture is merely the writing down of Revelation.[29] Revelation existed before its recording in Scripture,[30] it is not exhausted in the Scriptures,[31] and it continues in the Church through the inspiration of the Holy Spirit.[32] Scripture cannot, therefore, be used to test the faith of the Church, but must itself be judged by the faith of the Church.[33]

II

Although the Messenger comes to More armed only with the Scriptures—'learning enough for a Christian man'[34] most of the direct quotations and allusions in the Dialogue come from the lips of More himself.[35] Even if he considered the interpretation of Scripture to be subject to the Church, he was not about to cast himself as inferior to the Messenger in scriptural lore. Tunstall wished More to meet the Reformers' arguments squarely: 'for if you set yourself to refute something which they will say they never meant, all your labour will be in vain'.[36] More had decided, not without misgiving, to allow the Messenger to put the Reformers' case at some length.[37] Scriptural authority is adduced for all the positions maintained by the Reformers. There is nothing exceptional about this prooftext use of Scripture. More is merely acquainting his readers with the case he has to refute. We may infer something of More's fairness in expounding the Reformer's case from the fact that he does, in one important instance, allow a scriptural argument to be used that he does not explicitly answer. The Messenger argues against praying to saints on the ground that 'only Christ is our saviour and mediator to bring our nature again to God, and our only protector and advocate afore his Father'.[38] More does nothing to indicate the scriptural sources of this statement, even though its wording echoes those sources.[39] In fact, he never answers the argument directly, nor does he offer a Catholic interpretation of the texts on which it is based. Indeed, the heading of the following chapter declares:

> The author defereth the answer to the foresaid objections and first by scripture he proveth that the church of Christ cannot err in any necessary article of Christ's faith.[40]

There follows a discussion on the nature of the Church, its identity, inerrancy and its relationship with Scripture, which extends over the remaining fourteen chapters of the first book and the first seven chapters of the second book. At Book 2 Chapter 8,

> the author entereth the answer to the objections that have been before laid by the Messenger against the worship of images, and praying to saints, and going on pilgrimages.[41]

Here More makes ample use of Scripture in his defence of these practices, but he does not meet the central theological argument drawn from 1 Timothy 2:5 and 1 John 2:1. It is noteworthy that these passages are not referred to anywhere else in More's writings.[42] One of More's commonest responses to scriptural arguments against an orthodox position is to examine the texts and show that, properly understood, they do not serve the purpose the Reformers wish them to serve. In this case, More's reluctance to identify the scriptural authority, and his choice of this moment to introduce the lengthy and crucial discussion of the authority of the Church, suggest that he was embarrassed by this argument. He seems to have felt obliged to recognise it, but he does not allow it its full force, much less 'enforce yt and strength yt' of his own, as he was later to claim to have done in his dealing with his opponents' arguments.[43] When the question of relics, saints and pilgrimages was first raised, More was quick to announce that he would not dispute with those who claimed that the rejection of these practices by the Reformers was not heretical. He would not dispute it, firstly because he had 'no cunning in such matters', and secondly because, leaning and cleaving to the common faith 'as it best becometh a layman to do', he thereby plainly knew it for an heresy.⁴⁴ The discussion of the Church's relation to Scripture is central to More's position, and is not introduced merely to help him out of this particular difficulty. However, its incorporation into the work at just this point does enable him to conclude:

> Wherefore since I have proved you that the church cannot err in so great a point, nor, against the right faith, mistake the sentence of holy scripture ... I never need to go further or touch your texts or arguments to the contrary. For this side thus proved good, it must needs follow that the other side is nought.⁴⁵

III

In addition to the mere recording of the texts used by the Reformers, More shows either them or the Messenger using Scripture in a manner calculated to discredit them. There are several instances of this. In the argument against the 'costly ornament of the Church' the Messenger quotes the statement of the *Image of Love* that 'the money were ... better bestowed upon poor folk'.⁴⁶ More sees here an echo of the words of Judas at John 12:5, 'quare hoc ungentum non ueniit trecentis denariis, et datum est egenis?'.⁴⁷ In the synoptic parallels (Matthew 26: 8–9; Mark 14: 4–5) the question is attributed simply to 'discipuli' and 'quidam'. John's account is more useful to More's polemic:

> They might as well ask what good did that ointment to Christ's head. But the heretics grudge at the cost now, as their brother Judas did then, and say it were better spent in alms upon a poor folk; and this say many of them which can neither find in their hearts to spend upon the one nor the other.⁴⁸

More also points to the evils of an excessive literalism in interpreting Scripture. He tells the story of the preacher who, on the basis of Matthew 10: 34, declared that nowadays men preached not well the gospel . . . because he saw not the preachers persecuted, nor no strife nor business arise upon their preaching. Which things he said and wrote was the fruit of the gospel because Christ said, *Non veni pacem mittere sed gladium*.[49]

To the same purpose More tells the story of Bilney, who was

very fearful and scrupulous; and began at the first to fall into such a scrupulous holiness, that he reckoned himself bounden so straitly to keep and observe the words of Christ after the very letter that because our Lord biddeth us when we will pray enter into our chamber and shut the door to us, he thought it therefore sin to say his service abroad, and alway would be sure to have his chamber door shut unto him, while he said his matins.

Again, More brings the Messenger to assert that, faced with two conflicting passages of Scripture, he would use lots to decide between them, on the authority of the apostles, who at Acts 1:26 used lots to fill the place of Judas.[51] More suggests that Scripture can be made to serve any purpose by having the Messenger argue, with the aid of three scriptural quotations, that a man may perjure himself.[52] One of these texts is not to be found in the Bible, and G. Marc'hadour has suggested that this is a deliberate attempt to further ridicule rabid scripturalism.[53]

On two occasions the Messenger uses a verse from Scripture in a 'merry tale'.[54] R. Pineas suggests that More put most of the merry tales in the mouth of the Messenger in order to lower him in the esteem of his readers.[55] More himself castigates irreverence for the Scriptures, 'Which homely handling, as it proceedeth of little reverence, so doth it more and more engender in the mind a negligence and contempt of God's holy words'.[56] He incorporates the same argument in his halfhearted defence of the English bishops' reluctance to issue or approve a vernacular Bible. If the common people are to be allowed to interpret the Scriptures for themselves,

then should ye have the more blind the more bold, the more ignorant the more busy, the less wit the more inquisitive, the more fool the more talkative of great doubts and high questions of holy scripture, and of God's great and secret mysteries—and this, not soberly of any good affection, but presumptuously and unreverently at meat and at meal. And there, when the wine were in and the wit out, would they take upon them with foolish words and blasphemy to handle holy scripture in more homely manner than a song of Robin Hood.[57]

IV

More is as adept as his opponents in using proof-texts to establish his exposition of Catholic doctrine. Thus the heretic whose examination More reports in Book 4 gives in one place six texts to demonstrate that

> in faith and good works joined together, the good works were nothing worth, but that all the merit should be in the faith, and all the thank and reward should be given to the faith, and right nought to the good works.[58]

More answers this with eight texts demonstrating that

> in them, which after baptism, have time and reason to work well, good works must walk with faith, and sorrow at heart for fault of good works, if that faith shall aught avail them.[59]

In such instances as these, both sides are urging their strongest scriptural arguments. Because they are strong they are presented in the literal sense and without extravagant interpretation.

V

In More's critique of the Reformers' biblical arguments four methods can be distinguished. The first is to attend to the precise wording of the text to establish what is in fact prohibited, commanded or asserted, and what is left undetermined. The second is to examine the context to establish whether an inference drawn from the text is valid. The third is to cite other texts relevant to the argument. The fourth is to invalidate the Reformers' interpretation by reference to historical events recorded in the Scriptures. The method is basically Erasmian, but More might as easily be employing the techniques of legal argument. J. M. Headley has drawn attention to the importance of More's legal training in assessing his polemical method, and other commentators have noted obliquely the juridical framework of the *Dialogue*.[60] A passage in the Dialogue suggests that part of More's methodology has its origin in legal hermeneutics. In his reply to the Messenger's claim that worship of images had been forbidden by a law of Saint Gregory, More writes:

> I took down off a shelf among my books the register of Saint Gregory's Epistles, and therein turned to the very words which are by Graciane taken out of his second epistle *ad Serenum episcopum Massilie[nsis]*, and incorporate in the decrees. And then caused I him to read the formal words as they be couched in the decree. And, by the collation of the one with the tother, I caused him to see that Graciane had taken but a part of the epistle, and that by other words of the epistle itself it appeareth evidently that Saint Gregory spake of none other worship to be withdrawn from images but only divine worship and observance due to God, as by divers other things in the epistle appeareth plain.[61]

More can frequently be seen using the precise definition of the limits to which a text can be taken in his refutation of the reformers' arguments. Thus, when the Messenger refers to John 4: 21–23 to support the argument against pilgrimages by suggesting that 'very worshippers should worship in spirit and in truth, not in the hill, or in Jerusalem or any other temple of stone',[62] More replies that this interpretation is not supported by the text. He places the saying in a historical context and claims that Jesus said the time would come 'in which they should neither worship God in that hill of Gezera, nor in Jerusalem neither' simply because those places would be physically destroyed and 'the pagan manner of worshipping of the one, and the Jews' manner of worshipping in the other, turned both into the manner of worshipping of Christian faith and religion'. The text does not explicitly prohibit temple worship: 'Yet said he not to her that they should never after worship God in none other temple'. He establishes the validity of his limitation of the meaning by citing another text (Matthew 6:6) in which a similar limitation seems to him obviously necessary:

> this excludeth not that besides that he will be worshipped in his holy temple, no more than when he gave counsel that for avoiding of vainglory a man shall not stand and pray in the street to gather worldly praise but rather secretly pray in his chamber. This counsel forbad not the Jews, to whom he gave it, that they should never after come into the temple and pray.

More clinches his argument by citing a historical case that indicates that the Messenger's interpretation cannot be correct:

> I trow no man doubteth but that Christ's apostles were holy temples of God in their souls and well understood the words of their master ... But they not in their master's days only, but also after his resurrection, and after that they had received the holy ghost and were by him instructed of every truth longing to the necessity of their salvation, were not content only to pray secretly by themself in their chambers, but also resorted to the temple to make their prayers. And in that place, as a place pleasant to God, did they pray in spirit and in truth as well appeareth in the book of saint Luke written of the acts of Christ's holy apostles.[63]

This example of More's exegesis incorporates the four characteristic features of his manner of dealing with the arguments of the Reformers. Similar cases involving one, some or all of these features abound in the *Dialogue*.

VI

It is interesting to note that while More employs this critical hermeneutic to impugn the Reformers' arguments, he is able to ignore it when it suits him in the elaboration of his own position, and to advance strained, tendentious interpretations that would not survive his own critique.

Although More uses allegory sparingly, the Messenger appears to avoid it altogether. At times More cites patristic authority for his allegorization.[64] However, for his most extraordinary use of allegory he neither gives his patristic source nor acknowledges that he is employing an interpretation far from the literal sense. In his defence of the Church's right to impose laws on its members beyond those sanctioned in Scripture, More allegorizes the parable of the Samaritan.

> What meaneth it then that our Lord in the parable of the Samaritan, bearing the wounded man into the Inn of his Church, and delivering him to the host after that himself had dressed his wounds with wine and oil, and left with the host the two groats of the two testaments, and promised the host beside, that whatsoever the host would bestow upon him more, he would when he came again recompense him therefore.[65]

Quite apart from the arbitrariness of this interpretation, More suggests that it is the only interpretation. Erasmus, in the *Ratio Verae Theologiae*, scorned just this tendency to forget the obvious meaning of a narrative while seeking out frivolous allegories that could be used to shore up dogmas.[66]

In Book 2 More again misuses a parable. Defending the intercession of saints he asks,

> If the rich man that lay in hell . . . had a cure and care of his five brethren, were it likely that saints, then being so full of blessed charity in heaven, will nothing care for their brethren in Christ whom they see here in this wretched world?[67]

More ignores the obvious point of the story of Lazarus and sees it as teaching that the damned have 'carnal love and fleshly favour' towards their kin—a notion that serves no other purpose than allowing More to extrapolate to the greater charity of the saints.

When it suits his purpose, More is prepared to ignore the exegetical technique of collation and comparison of texts. In his argument against the Messenger's fear that miracles may be feigned, More states:

> Christ among Christian people suffereth not such things to happen oft, nor such delusion to last long, but shortly to their shame, as it hath appeared in some, doth utter and make open their falsehood as himself said of all such: That ye whisper one in another's ear shall be preached out aloud upon the ridge of the house roof.[68]

More does not give the source of this quotation. It is plain, however, that he has in mind Luke 12:3, where this remark follows a warning by Christ against the hypocrisy of the Pharisees. More could have established by means of collation and comparison that the remark refers not to the Pharisees and their hypocrisy, but to Christ's disciples and their preaching. At Matthew 10: 26–27, where the remark is also recorded, there is no possibility of ambiguity. More would have done better to have quoted Luke 12: 2, 'there is nothing covered that shall not be revealed; nothing hidden that shall not be known', which might be taken as a reference to the hypocrisy of the Pharisees. However, this saying also occurs in slightly different wording in Luke 8: 17, where it is associated with the parable of the lamp, and More conflates this with another Lucan version of this parable (Luke 11: 33) and with Matthew 10: 26–27 and Luke 12: 49 to defend the Church against the Reformers' notion of a secret, unknown Church:

> And he would have his faith divulged and spread abroad openly, not alway whispered in hugger-mugger. And therefore he bound his preachers to stand thereby and not to revoke his word for no pain. For he said that he did not light the candle to put it and hide it under a bushel; for so would no man do; but he had kindled a fire which he would not should lie and smoulder as coals doth in quench; but he would it should burn and give light.[69]

More could not have been blamed for using the 'nothing is hidden' saying for two purposes when Luke himself has done this. But More fails to keep the two contexts separate. In fact, in the passage just quoted, he has also conflated Luke 12: 3. 'Whispered in hugger-mugger' has no foundation in Luke 11: 33 or 8: 17, but it does take up 'quod in aurem locuti estis in cubiculis' in Luke 12: 3, which More rendered 'that ye whisper one in another's ear' and which he applied to the hypocrisy of the Pharisees and of those who feign miracles.[70]

One of More's extraordinary uses of Scripture seems all the odder in that he undercuts his own argument. To demonstrate Mary's perpetual virginity, More tries to show from Scripture that she had taken a vow of virginity and then to infer that she would not have broken such a vow after the birth of Christ: 'for surely whoso considereth the words of the gospel, in saint Luke, shall well perceive that she had vowed virginity'.[71] His argument for the vow of virginity is established by exacting the maximum of meaning from Mary's reply to the angel's message at Luke 1: 31 – 'Lo, thou shalt conceive in thy womb and bring forth a child, and thou shalt call his name Jesus.' More reasons that if the angel had used the present tense, 'Lo, thou art conceived', Mary would have reason for replying 'How may this be? For as for man, I know none.' Since the angel used the future tense, he argues, the remark could only have caused surprise if she had vowed herself to virginity. The trouble with this argument is that Mary's reply is in the present tense, when it too ought to be in the future. More foresees and meets this objection by pointing out that in such matters English women frequently use the present tense when they mean the future:

> after the manner of speaking; by which a nun might say, 'As for man there meddleth none with me,' signifying that never there shall. And in common speech is that figure much in use, by which a woman saith of one who she is determined never to marry, 'We may well talk together but we wed not together,' meaning that they never shall wed together.[72]

In all of this More overlooks the significance of Mary's betrothal to Joseph at Luke 1: 27. Having gone to such pains with this twisted exegesis to show that 'appeareth it evidently that she had then a full determined purpose of virginity',[73] More then observes, 'this reverent article of our Lady's perpetual virginity, the church of Christ, being taught the truth by Christ, perpetually hath believed since the time of Christ. And yet is there no word thereof in Christ's gospel written.'[74]

In his defence of clerical celibacy, More asserts that 'in the old law given to Moses, the priests of the temple for the time of their ministration forbare their own house and the company of their wives'.[75] More might have argued a case for this by putting together several ordinances of the book of Leviticus, but he infers it surprisingly and improbably from the story of the annunciation of the birth of John the Baptist in Luke 1. There it is said that it was the turn of Zechariah's section to serve in the temple. More postulates the continence of the priests during the time of the ministration as the explanation of their taking it in turns to serve in the temple.

Among the principal causes of More's distaste for Tyndale's new Testament was its failure to render the word *presbyteros* by 'priest'.[76] Tyndale's doctrine, or rather lack of a doctrine, of order did require comment by More.[77] But in his polemic, More unjustly accuses Tyndale of duplicity in his translation. More writes:

> wheresoever the scripture speaketh of the Priests that were among the Jews, there doth he in his translation call them still by the name of priests. But wheresoever the scripture speaketh of the priests of Christ's church, there doth he put away the name of priest ... [and] make it seem that the scripture did never speak of any priests different from laymen among Christian people.[78]

Tyndale's use of 'senior' to translate *presbyteros* was certainly tendentious, but it was not deceitful. In the New Testament the Jewish priests and high priests are *hiereis* and *archiereis*.[79] In the Christian context, *archiereus* is used only of Jesus himself,[80] while *hiereus* and its congnates are used either of Jesus or of the whole body of believers.[81] Among the ministers of the Christian church are *episkopoi, presbyteroi* and *diakonoi*,[82] but never *hiereis*. In the literal sense the New Testament does not speak of any priests different from laymen among Christian people.

VII

In this investigation of More's use of Scripture I have drawn attention to its peculiarities, but I do not wish to suggest that his use of Scripture is more frequently than not at variance with his own and Erasmus's hermeneutic. Nevertheless, I think it does emerge that More does not consistently use Scripture in accordance with any theory of the way it may be legitimately used. Where the manifest sense of a text will help him to contradict an opponent's argument, or to confirm traditional teaching, he does, of course, employ it. At the same time, however, he seems quite ready to employ a text when its utility derives from its being read out of context, or even distorted in meaning. By the nature of the controversy, Scripture was a major authority, and More seems to have been determined to have it always and only on his side.

The hermeneutical devices that More takes from Erasmus are subservient to a far more fundamental principle of exegesis, and can be used or ignored as the exigencies of his polemic require. Since More believed nothing in Scripture could be found to condemn the teaching of the Church, he could confidently reject all the arguments of the Reformers in advance.[83] The truth of the Church's doctrine depended on an *a priori* principle, not upon the vigour of the arguments in its favour, nor upon the real success with which opposing arguments could be met.

There is rather more of the defence lawyer than of the Erasmian exegete in the *Dialogue*. It is unlikely that Tunstall would have been displeased with the outcome, for another of his reasons for commissioning More was his 'habit of championing catholic truth most keenly in every discussion'.[84]

Notes

1. 'Licence for Sir Thomas More to keep and read heretical books, 7 March 1528', in *English Historical Documents*, vol. V: 1485–1558, edited by C. H. Williams (London: Eyre and Spottiswoode, 1971), pp. 828–9.

2. *Opus Epistolarum Desiderii Erasmi Roterodami*, edited by P. S. Allen, vol. V (Oxford: 1924), pp. 290–3.
3. *De Veritate Corporis et Sanguinis Domini nostri Jesu Christi in Eucharistia* (1551), Paris: 1554; *Contra Blasphematores Dei praedestinationis opus*, Antwerp: 1555; cf. *Dictionary of National Biography* (Compact Edition, Oxford University Press, 1975), vol. II, pp. 2119 (1240), 2120 (1241).
4. *Opus Epistolarum Erasmi*, vol. II, p. 603; cf. *Dictionary of National Biography*, vol. II, p. 2119 (1238).
5. G. Marc'hadour, *The Bible in the Works of Thomas More* (Nieuwkoop: 1972), vol. IV, pp. 33–4.
6. The work is known by the short titles *The Dialogue Concerning Tyndale* and *The Dialogue Concerning Heresies*. In these notes it will be indicated by *Dialogue*. Reference will be to the modern version of W. E. Campbell in *The Dialogue Concerning Tyndale by Sir Thomas More* (London: Eyre and Spottiswoode, 1927).
7. *Dialogue*, p. 2.
8. 'Well, said I, then since I am already married twice, and therefore never can be priest, and ye be so set in mind of marriage that ye never will be priest, we two be not the most metely to ponder what might be said in this matter for the priestes part.' *Dialogue*, p. 25.
9. *Dialogue*, p. 214.
10. *Dialogue*, p. 249.
11. *Ratio seu Methodus Compendio Perveniendi ad Veram Theologiam*, in *Desiderii Erasmi Roterodami Opera Omnia*, recognovit Joannes Clericus (Leiden: 1704), Tomus V, col. 778. This work will hereafter be cited as *Ratio*.
12. *Dialogue*, p. 84.
13. *Dialogue*, p. 102.
14. *Dialogue*, pp. 246–7.
15. *Dialogue*, p. 250.
16. *Dialogue*, p. 73.
17. *Dialogue*, p. 11.
18. *Dialogue*, p. 11.
19. *Ratio*, col. 75–84.
20. *Dialogue*, pp. 75, 284–5; *Ratio*, col. 131A–C.
21. *Dialogue*, p. 82; *Ratio*, col. 79C–D.
22. *Dialogue*, p. 83; *Ratio*, Col. 76A.
23. *Dialogue*, p. 83; *Ratio*, col. 80F–82A.
24. *Dialogue*, p. 83; *Ratio*, col. 128B.
25. *Dialogue*, p. 83; *Ratio*, col. 131A–C; 77E–79C.
26. *Ratio*, col. 76E.
27. *Ratio*, col. 128B.
28. *Dialogue*, p. 87.
29. *Dialogue*, pp. 95–6.
30. *Dialogue*, p. 74.
31. *Dialogue*, pp. 96, 98–9.

32. *Dialogue*, pp. 98; 121–2.
33. *Dialogue*, p. 130; cf. pp. 95–6.
34. *Dialogue*, p. 11.
35. This can be gauged by working through the list of scriptural references and allusions in the *Dialogue* provided by G. Marc'hadour in *The Bible in the Works of Thomas More*, vol. V, pp. 179–82.
36. *English Historical Documents*, vol. V, p. 829.
37. *Dialogue*, p. 2.
38. *Dialogue*, p. 60.
39. cf. 1 Timothy 2:5 and 1 John 2:1.
40. *Dialogue*, p. 63.
41. *Dialogue*, p. 147.
42. Marc'hadour, *The Bible in the Works of Thomas More*, vol. III, pp. 128, 175. At *Dialogue* p. 25, the Messenger quotes St Paul to the effect that we have Christ 'for our advocate afore the Father'. This is much closer to 1 John 2:1 than to 1 Timothy 2:5. W. E. Campbell (footnote, ad loc.) suggests a reference to Romans 8:34.
43. *The Apologye of Syr Thomas More Knyght*, edited with an introduction and notes by A. I. Taft (London: 1930), p. 5.
44. *Dialogue*, p. 14.
45. *Dialogue*, pp. 146–7.
46. *Dialogue*, p. 16.
47. The question of the source of More's biblical references is involved. J. M. Headley (*Responsio ad Lutherum, The Yale Edition of the Complete Works of St Thomas More*, vol. V, part II, New Haven: 1969, pp. 822–3) found that in the *Responsio ad Lutherum* More often quoted Scripture from memory and that in addition to the Vulgate he used the Old Latin Version and Erasmus's New Testament. Where it has been necessary to cite a text alluded to or translated by More I have used J. Wordsworth and H. J. White, *Novum Testamentum Latine, secundum editionem Sancti Hieronymi* (editio minor, curante H. I. White; London: The British and Foreign Bible Society).
48. *Dialogue*, p. 23.
49. *Dialogue*, p. 81.
50. *Dialogue*, p. 184; cf. Matthew 6:6.
51. *Dialogue*, pp. 104–7.
52. *Dialogue*, p. 203.
53. G. Marc'hadour, *The Bible in the Works of Thomas More*, vol. I, p. 184.
54. *Dialogue*, pp. 52–3, 216.
55. R. Pineas, *Thomas More and Tudor Polemics* (London: 1968), p. 92.
56. *Dialogue*, p. 251.
57. *Dialogue*, p. 246.
58. *Dialogue*, pp. 289–90.
59. *Dialogue*, pp. 290–2.

60. 'Thomas More and Luther's Revolt', in *Archiv für Reformationsgeschichte*, 60 (1969) 145–190, p. 146. Cf. L. A. Schuster, 'Thomas More's Polemical Career: 1523–1533', in *The Yale Edition of the Complete Works of St Thomas More*, vol. VIII, *The Confutation of Tyndale's Answer* (New Haven: 1973), p. 1261; J. Gairdner, *Lollardy and the Reformation in England: An Historical Survey* (London: 1908), vol. I, p. 515. C. S. Lewis (*English Literature in the Sixteenth Century, excluding Drama*, Oxford: 1944, p. 172) felt that 'a lawyer . . . ought to have had something more pertinent to say about the whole nature of evidence'.
61. *Dialogue*, pp. 262, 264.
62. *Dialogue*, p. 29.
63. *Dialogue*, p. 30; cf. Acts 2:46.
64. *Dialogue*, pp. 87, 244.
65. *Dialogue*, pp. 65–66; cf. Luke 10: 33–37.
66. *Ratio*, col 126A–B.
67. *Dialogue*, p. 148; cf. Luke 16: 27–28.
68. *Dialogue*, p. 55.
69. *Dialogue*, pp. 140–1.
70. *Dialogue*, p. 55.
71. *Dialogue*, p. 100.
72. *Dialogue*, p. 100.
73. *Dialogue*, p. 101.
74. *Dialogue*, p. 101.
75. *Dialogue*, p. 228.
76. *Dialogue*, p. 207.
77. cf. E. Fleesman-van Leer, 'The Controversy about Ecclesiology between Thomas More and William Tyndale', in *Nederlands Archief voor Kerkgeschiedenis*, N. S. 44 (1960–1961) 65–86, pp. 79–81.
78. *Dialogue*, p. 210.
79. e.g. Mark 1: 44; Matthew 26: 51.
80. e.g. Hebrews 2:17.
81. e.g. Hebrews 7: 21; Revelation 1: 6, 5: 10, 20: 6; 1 Peter 2: 5, 9.
82. e.g. Philippians 1: 1; 1 Timothy 3: 8, 5: 17.
83. *Dialogue*, pp. 79, 96.
84. *English Historical Documents*, vol. V, p. 828.

DIALOGUE OF COMFORT FOR WHOM?
MAUREEN PURCELL O.P.

It may seem temerarious for a medievalist to come among you to talk of such an important work of Thomas More as the *Dialogue of Comfort*, much less to hint, as I shall surely do, that this is a work instinct with the 'mind of the Middle Ages', expressing a firm conviction of the continuity of Christian spirituality in the face of an imminent and devastating threat of new ways of thought, new approaches to God and religion. There is a world of difference between the humanist More of the *Utopia* and the traditionalist More of the Tower works.

More has often been accused, *inter alia*, of failing to read the signs of the times and of obstinately trying to turn back the clock, of being at least arch-conservative, if not reactionary. A clear-sighted More, it is implied, would have accepted the new political and religious realities as he showed a capacity for doing in the *Utopia* and in his own political actions, and would have been speedy to out-Cromwell Cromwell, a less clever man than he. Then the King's mistress should not have had the opportunity, or indeed the necessity, to 'delight Henry with her dancing until she danced off More's Head'.[1]

Instead, More remained an anomaly, a man of no noticeable influence, his Lord Chancellorship a negative interval before modernity bustled him out of the way. Thus more than one eminent Tudor historian. More, the outmoded, the man who missed the boat to the new world because he chose to founder with the barque of Peter; and this choice not so much the outcome of positive intellectual conviction as from inability to adjust to changing times. This foundering with the Petrine barque, which is effective reason for the writing of the *Dialogue of Comfort*, is an awkward thing for those who puzzle over More's ultimate decision seemingly to abandon his conciliarist position and to abide by the principle of papal supremacy and, by logical extension, of papal primacy.[2] More does not raise the question in his *Dialogue of Comfort* because his concern there is rather with his relationship with God, in the light of various temptations, than with the validity of the particular cause he has espoused. This is clear even in his treatment of the need for Christian unity if the Turkish threat is to be overcome. He stresses the view for unity and refrains from polemics because his preoccupation is with a different level of truth.

If we think of the better-known popes during More's lifetime we cannot help being amazed by the sacrifice that the defence of the principle demanded of his sound common sense. No wonder even his family boggled. There was Alexander VI, whom Savonarola had declared no pope for his unworthiness, and whose licentiousness drove that same Savonarola to revive the Joachimite vision of an Angelic Pope to come. No angels Alexander's successors however: Julius II, of whom it is enough to say he merited a place of honour in Machiavelli's realistic princely rogue's gallery, and Leo X, whose portrait by Giulio Romano sufficiently witnesses to his thraldom to sensuality.

How *could* More put aside his conciliarist notions and, a solitary layman, uphold the supremacy of an office of whose degradation he was all too aware? In viewing More's earlier reforming zeal, his attacks on corruption, we might well expect a less than unconditional surrender of his critical faculties. That is to forget the More who thought of being a Carthusian (or an Observant Friar), who went on pilgrimage, who prayed, fasted and meditated according to the customs of his fathers. I venture to suggest that the comfort that More saw as a possible consequence of his *Dialogue* was the spiritually challenging reconciliation of these two attitudes of mind. His determination in prison was to see his position clearly, and to see it whole, to blink at nothing and to be satisfied only when his soul was bare to himself and his intimate circle, as he surely knew it was to God.

This is the comfort, bear it who may, of absolute intellectual integrity, of joy in conformity with Christ's Passion and of relaxation into the anticipated joys of heaven only after that, only as a reward for conformity to Christ crucified.

Perhaps the mistake that the medievalist might most easily make in looking at More's spiritual testament is to try too hard to fit it into the traditional spiritual writings of the Middle Ages, the *Consolatio*, the *Ars moriendi*, or the more diverse and sometimes more personal writings of the mystics. I am not sure that this is a great danger; no-one could mistake More's *Dialogue of Comfort* for what it is—an original if loosely organized piece of work, which for sheer revelation of personality is rivalled earlier, and perhaps only, by More's own countrywomen, the anchoress Julian of Norwich and the adamantly undomestic housewife Margery Kempe. Though More was obviously steeped in the spiritual writings of the later Middle Ages, the *Dialogue of Comfort* is a highly personal work, and one that clearly reflects the writer's circumstances and preoccupations as the work of Mother Julian reflects the serenity of hers, or that of Meister Eckhart the controversial ambivalence of his.

I am not sure why it is that Professor Elton should expect spiritual writers to conform to patterns and formulae, but that is indeed the impression he gives in his recent review of the Yale edition of the *Dialogue of Comfort Against Tribulation*.[3] I was more than delighted to find that my agreement with Professor Elton's remarks on the *Dialogue* (as opposed to the edition) was very slender indeed. Elton notes in the review that More did not produce in the *Dialogue of Comfort* a work of meditation, nor yet of mysticism, but one of purely homiletic content. Here, he says, is neither philosophy nor theology, but simple instruction.[4] More, according to Elton's judgement, was never a mystic. Now I find all this indicative of a very odd approach indeed; I should go so far as to say I find it the expression of a marked spiritual insensitivity. It reminds me of a dialogue I once had with a young English cleric who maintained that *Piers Plowman* could not possibly be considered a work of mysticism because its categories do not conform to those of the scholastic theologians.

What I think we have in the *Dialogue of Comfort* is the work of a mind whose undeniably rich spiritual texture shows itself as the product of a lifetime of meditation on the Scriptures, the Fathers and post-patristic works of spirituality. It is a fine point to say that the *Dialogue* is not meditative because, unlike other works before it, except perhaps *Piers Plowman*, it has not a rigorously ecclesiastical setting. The *Dialogue*, that is to say, takes place between two laymen, and is concerned with the practical application, in a real world of secular concerns, of the spiritual principles under discussion. More's *Dialogue* is as theological as its medieval precedents— the many dialogues and debates represented by their authors, such as Ramon Lull, as taking place between clerics and either Jews or Arabs, or between confessors and their penitents, between spiritual directors and those whom they directed. I am not at all sure what Professor Elton understands by theology, but I am sure that he applies a wrong notion of it to the *Dialogue of Comfort*. Indeed, I suspect that it is his notion of theology and sin that leads him to his perverse judgement that More's obsession was with sex.[5] Like Freud, he appears to be oblivious of the categories, if not the existence, of the other six deadly sins. Perhaps one ought to remind oneself that study of constitutional documents is not good preparation for spiritual judgements.

More was well acquainted with the writings of Walter Hilton, who in his *Scale of Perfection* allowed for the participation of those leading an active life in the contemplative way.[6] If he did not adopt that idea directly from Hilton, he must certainly have met it in Aquinas.[7] In the *Dialogue* he was not concerned with a general discussion of man's relationship with God, but rather with his personal need to realign his own relationship with God in the light of changed circumstances. This is not to say that More's treatise has no universal application. On the contrary, though the case More takes from the Turkish threat to Christendom is, on the surface, a restricted and very specific one, its basic notion is of universal application. This notion is that one must face every serious temptation as a new experience, building on past experience, certainly, but exercising the utmost courage and vigilance in analysing the dangers ahead, and taking the most humanly realistic view of one's own frailty and weakness. Above all, one must rely, not on one's own previously acquired strengths, but on victory in Christ, a victory paradoxically resting on a lifetime of spiritual self-discipline and yet not certain until the end; then, too, the victory is that of Christ crucified whose pains shame us out of wishing an easy way to heaven.[8]

If there is one characteristic of More that is outstanding in the *Dialogue* it is his sense of responsibility to God for graces given, and his corresponding urge to shirk no jot of that responsibility. It is this responsibility that drives More on to examine every possible way in which he, or others, might be beguiled into betraying God and his gifts, into substituting a lesser good for eternal bliss. In part the comfort of the *Dialogue* is to be found in More's own sense of relief at dangers explored and considered at their worst.

Before I pass on from Professor Elton's review altogether, let me make one further remark about his assessment of the *Dialogue*: Elton considers, understandably, that the autobiographical element in the *Dialogue* has been exaggerated.[9] It is not hard to see that it would barely accord with Elton's latest theory about More's sex obsession to accord the *Dialogue of Comfort* autobiographical status. This would obviously mean that More, on the very brink of death, was so dishonest as not to discuss his besetting temptation, or else that he did not, in fact, suffer unduly from that temptation. Since Elton claims that More was motivated rather by excessive fear of hell than by anticipated bliss in heaven,[10] this means the Professor is in a dilemma that he either fails to recognize or hopes not to have detected.

Here, in this idea of More's excessive fear of hell, we have a clue to what sometimes goes wrong with analyses of More's spiritual drift in *A Dialogue of Comfort Against Tribulation*. What emerges from the *Dialogue* to anyone aware of the tradition of Christian exegesis and spiritual writing is an expression of More's deep sense of sin; not an excessive fear of hell, but a possibly over-active sense of sin, fostered by the religious pre-occupations that, at this very time, led on the one hand to Luther's basic protest in favour of justification by faith and on the other to Calvin's protest in favour of the harsher doctrine of the elect. For anyone well acquainted with the serener, though no less realistic, view of sin of a Julian of Norwich, it is perhaps all too easy to overemphasize the grimness of More's *Dialogue*, with its dark view of the endless and senseless capacity of human beings for the self-betrayal of sin.

It is clear, if we read him carefully, that More is as sure as Mother Julian that all shall be well. He can, without reserve, hope to meet his false judges and his jailer merrily in heaven;[11] he can see that, having preserved the integrity of his conscience, a man may 'leese his head and have none harme'.[12] But in the *Dialogue of Comfort* More expresses a theology of temptation and sin that has none of the immediacy of consolation of Mother Julian's.

In an echo of Augustine's *O felix culpa*, Mother Julian muses on the idea that sin is behovable. In her thirteenth Revelation[13] she writes:

> And thus, in my folly, afore this time often I wondered why by the great foreseeing wisdom of God the beginning of sin was not letted: for then, methought, all should have been well . . .
> But Jesus . . . answered by this word and said: *It behoved that there should be sin; but all shall be well, and all shall be well, and all manner of thing shall be well.*
> In this naked word *sin*, our Lord brought to my mind, generally, *all that is not good*, and the shameful despite and the utter noughting that He bare for us in this life, and His dying; and all the pains and passions of all His creatures, ghostly and bodily; (for we be all partly noughted, and we shall be noughted following our Master, Jesus, till we be full purged, that is to say, till we be fully noughted of our deadly flesh and of all our inward affections which are not very good;) and the beholding of this, with all pains that ever were or ever shall be,—and with all these I understand the Passion of Christ for most pain, and overpassing. All this was shewed in a touch and quickly passed over into comfort: for our good Lord would not that the soul were affeared of this terrible sight . . .
> And thus pain, *it* is something, as to my sight, for a time; for it purgeth, and maketh us to know ourselves and to ask mercy. For the

Passion of our Lord is comfort to us against all this, and so is His blessed will. And for the tender love that our good Lord hath to all that shall be saved, He comforteth readily and sweetly, signifying thus: *It is sooth that sin is cause of all this pain; but all shall be well, and all shall be well, and all manner [of] thing shall be well.*

These words were said full tenderly, showing no manner of blame to me nor to any that shall be saved. Then were it a great unkindness to blame or wonder on God for my sin, since He blameth not me for sin.

And in these words I saw a marvellous high mystery hid in God, which mystery He shall openly make known to us in Heaven: in which knowing we shall verily see the cause why He suffered sin to come. In which sight we shall endlessly joy in our Lord God.[14]

Thus I saw how Christ hath compassion on us for the cause of sin . . . I was fulfilled, in part, with compassion of all mine even-Christians —for that well, well beloved people that shall be saved. For God's servants, Holy Church, shall be shaken in sorrow and anguish, tribulation in this world, as men shake a cloth in the wind.

And as to this our Lord answered in this manner: *A great thing shall I make hereof in Heaven of endless worship and everlasting joys.*

Yea, so far forth I saw, that our Lord joyeth of the tribulations of His servants, with ruth and compassion. On each person that He loveth, to His bliss for to bring [them], He layeth something that is no blame in His sight, whereby they are blamed and despised in this world, scorned, mocked, and outcasted. And this He doeth for to hinder the harm that they should take from the pomp and the vainglory of this wretched life, and make their way ready to come to Heaven, and up-raise them in His bliss everlasting. For He saith: *I shall wholly break you of your vain affections and your vicious pride; and after that I shall together gather you, and make you mild and meek, clean and holy, by oneing to me.*

And then I saw that each kind compassion that man hath on his even-Christians with charity, it is Christ in him . . .

In His Passion . . . [and] in this Compassion . . . were two manner of understandings in our Lord's meaning. The one was the bliss that we are brought to, wherein He willeth that we rejoice. The other is for comfort in our pain: for He willeth that we perceive that it shall all be turned to worship and profit by virture of His passion, that we perceive that we suffer not alone but with Him, and see Him to be our Ground, and that we see His pains and His noughting passeth so

> far all that we may suffer, that it may not be fully thought.
>
> The beholding of this will save us from mumuring and despair in the feeling of our pains. And if we see soothly that our sin deserveth it, yet His love excuseth us, and of His great courtesy He doeth away all our blame, and beholdeth us with ruth and pity as children innocent and unloathful.[15]
>
> But in this I stood beholding things general, troublously and mourning, saying thus to our Lord in my meaning, with full great dread: *Ah! good Lord, how might all be well, for the great hurt that is come, by sin, to the creature?* And here I desired, as far as I durst, to have some more open declaring wherewith I might be eased in this matter.
>
> And to this our blessed Lord answered full meekly and with full lovely cheer, and shewed that Adam's sin was the most harm that ever was done, or ever shall be, to the world's end; and also He shewed that this [sin] is openly known in all Holy Church on earth. Furthermore He taught that I should behold the glorious Satisfaction: for this Amends-making is more pleasing to God and more worshipful, without comparison, than ever was the sin of Adam harmful. Then signifieth our blessed Lord thus in this teaching, that we should take heed to this: *For since I have made well the most harm, then it is my will that thou know thereby that I shall make well all that is less.*[16]

In her view man's necessary sense of sin is subsumed in an overwhelming awareness of God's love upholding and sustaining the sinner.

> This is a sovereign friendship of our courteous Lord that He keepeth us so tenderly while we be in sin; and furthermore He toucheth us full privily and sheweth us our sin by the sweet light of mercy and grace. But when we see our self so foul, then ween we that God were wroth with us for our sin, and then are we stirred of the Holy Ghost by contrition unto prayer and desire for the amending of our life with all our mights, to slacken the wrath of God, unto the time we find a rest in soul and a softness in conscience. Then hope we that God hath forgiven us our sins: and it is truth. And then sheweth our courteous Lord Himself to the soul—well-merrily and with glad cheer— with friendly welcoming as if it had been in pain and in prison, saying sweetly thus: *My darling I am glad thou art come to me: in all thy*

woe I have ever been with thee; and now seest thou my loving and we be oned in bliss. Thus are sins forgiven by mercy and grace, and our soul is worshipfully received in joy like as it shall be when it cometh by the gracious working of the Holy Ghost and the virtue of Christ's Passion.

Here understand I in truth that all manner of things are made ready for us by the great goodness of God, so far forth that what time we be ourselves in peace and charity, we be verily saved. But because we may not have this in fulness while we are here, therefore it falleth to us overmore to live in sweet prayer and lovely longing with our Lord Jesus. For He longeth ever to bring us to the fulness of joy;...[17]

More's sense of sin tends to a starker reality, which at times in the *Dialogue* seems near to overwhelming him. He seems almost driven to forget, and nowhere I should suggest more than in his merry jests, that God's wrath is a thing of man's imagery, not residing in God. In this More's *Dialogue* shows clearly its origins in a different spiritual climate, closer to the anguished soul-searching of an Ignatius. It is only in the warm personal overtones that the *Dialogue of Comfort* is lifted above the severity that underlies its argument.

It would be a most interesting exercise to compare the *Dialogue* closely with Julian's *Revelations* for there are many striking similarities, by reason of a common tradition and almost despite the strong spiritual individuality of each writer. Take an example. While Mother Julian sees sin as behovable,[18] More takes up Augustine's notion and with a delightful twist has the young Vincent wonder why it is that, with tribulation so spiritually fruitful and prosperity so perilous, men should seek to avoid tribulation.

Vincent

But yet good vncle though that some do thus/this answereth not full the mater/For we se that the whole church in the comen seruice, vse diuers colletes/in which all men pray specially for the princes and prelattes, & generally euery man for other, & for hym selfe to/that god wold vouchsafe to send them all perpetuall helth & prosperitie/

> And I can se no good man pray god send an other sorow, nor no such praers are there put in the prestes portuouse as far as I can here/
>
> And yet yf it were as you say good vncle/that perpetuall prosperitie were to the sowle so perilouse, & tribulacion therto so frutefull/than were as me semeth euery man bound of charitie, not onely to pray god send their neibours sorow/but also to help therto them selfe/& when folke are sike, not pray god send them helth/but when they come to comfort them [they shuld say] I am glad good gossep/that ye be so syk/I pray god kepe you long therin/and neyther shuld any man give any medicyne to other/nor take any medicyn hym selfe neyther/for by the mynyshyng of the tribulacion, he taketh away part of the profit from his sowle, which can by no bodely profit be sufficiently recumpensid.[19]

Both here and elsewhere one can see that More has taken the abstract consideration of the fall as a happy fault drawing God's son from heaven for man's redemption, and has turned the ancient paradox into a homely reaction that mocks such clever paradoxes at the same time as it makes use of them. More, who delighted in paradoxes, but who found his paradoxical situation a fresh challenge to his spiritual reserves, thus achieves a double irony.

Similarly we might compare in these two writers their treatment of the common theme of life as a prison and heaven as true liberty. While More's is an extended discussion ranging over every aspect of actual imprisonment and obstacles to liberty even without prison walls, Mother Julian deals with the subject in a few sentences.

> This place is prison and this life is penance, and in the remedy He willeth that we rejoice. The remedy is that our Lord is with us, keeping and leading into the fulness of joy. For this is an endless joy to us in our Lord's signifying, that He that shall be our bliss when we are there, He is our keeper while we are here.[20]

Does any of this bring us closer to judging why More wrote *A Dialogue of Comfort Against Tribulation*, and for whose comfort? If, as is claimed by many commentators, including his early biographers, More wrote the work for his family and intimate friends, then we ought to consider the nature of the comfort he offered in this testament. First of all we have to beware of accepting too uncritically family traditions, more especially of a hagiographical nature, since these flourish and develop apocryphal accretions with great rapidity. If this work *is* More's last testament designed as a comfort for his grieving family, it comes in a strange form, one that must have seared the hearts and consciences of those who had deserted him, betrayed his education, and even tempted him to go against his own conscience.

Did More write to instruct his family in the event of future and easily foreseeable dangers to their faith, and tests of their loyalty to their consciences? To answer this we must look beyond the work itself, which gives no direct statement of purpose, to the subsequent actions of the More family and circle of friends. The lesson they appear to have taken was not that of giving witness by martyrdom, but of avoiding the ultimate test by going into exile. Granted some members of the family later endured imprisonment and other penalties attached to recusancy, but the comfort they found seems rather to have been a retrospective understanding of More's position than a readiness to follow his example exactly.

Thus, I think the other question more pertinent. Did More write the *Dialogue* in order to reassure his family that he had arrived at his decision to resist even as far as death, slowly, and only after considerable conflict of mind and heart? This seems much more likely, but if it were so, we have still to decide why More chose to cast the record of his very personal struggles in such a form. Why choose a fictional dialogue between two Hungarians anticipating the troubles to come for Christians should the Turkish conquest spread over their whole land?

It seems to me somewhat irrelevant, perhaps even trivializing, to discuss at great length the equation of Hungary with England, of Islam with Protestantism—interesting, but irrelevant in this context. More's works do not elsewhere lead us to believe that the fiction, where he casts his work as fiction, is his prime consideration. True, he is careful to sustain the fiction by every means possible, and with all manner of pseudo-authentication. We find it in the *Utopia*; we find it in the *Dialogue of Comfort*; and yet I cannot believe in the specific fiction as more than a convenience, nor as intrinsic to the theme of *Comfort Against Tribulation*.

When thinking about More in prison we must never lose sight of the fact that he was a man accustomed to lively conversation, to sharing his thoughts with family and friends, and one thoroughly convinced of the need for constant growth through exchange of ideas. From this he was almost completely cut off by his imprisonment, and it is not a hard task to discern that More would make the best of his reduced social contact, in written communication. It is not accidental, I think, that the work we are discussing was cast in the form of a dialogue. More's ever lively sense of irony would lead him to appreciate the implications of making do with a feigned dialogue, especially such an unequally shared dialogue, where everyone would assume that the loquacious old man represented More himself. In this way the dialogue form may be seen as a comfort to the isolated prisoner himself.

It is easy to make the assumption that Antony is More, and Professor Elton does not avoid falling into a trap on this account. While he denies that the *Dialogue of Comfort* is largely autobiographical, Elton claims that Antony is the spokesman of More's settled and secure convictions. The work as he sees it is not concerned with a search for truth, but with the imparting of instruction based on More's experience and judgement.[21]

To think this way is to miss one of More's most skilful effects in the *Dialogue*. Though Antony is presented as having achieved wisdom by the experiences of a long and meditative life, behind him the sensitive reader must always be aware of the author, persistently questioning his own motives and assumptions. Antony may well voice his serene conclusions as if he had them all compact, all apprehended at one and the same time, but we are constantly aware of the author working piecemeal and in uncertainty for each separate conclusion.

While not wanting to move into the thickets of literary criticism with its types of ambiguity and its differing levels of communication, I think we must concede to More the skill of having maintained at least two levels of dialogue in his work. There is that between the two Hungarians, and there is that between More and his own soul. What Elton fails to see is the skill with which More manipulates the time lag between More's debate with himself and Anthony's steady enunciation of his seemingly longer-held wisdom.

What we must constantly bear in mind as well is that the *Dialogue of Comfort* is eminently a lawyer's book, exploring minutely each detail of the problem and letting no point go until his lawyer's mind is satisfied, his plea fully expounded and his case unassailable. It is this as much as the mode of composition that accounts for the rambling nature of the work and the seemingly tentative comfort achieved. More, in publishing his research by way of an interim report, seems to lag one step behind the Recording Angel in summing up his case.

It is this above all that seems to me to have constituted the possible comfort that More may have envisaged for his family —a grim comfort, which they must have needed great strength to accept and profit by. What they were treated to was the raw spectacle of More wrestling with his conscience and striving to reassemble his ideas and beliefs in an entirely new pattern. What More's family and friends could have seen would be More's accumulation of evidence to support his conviction that his chosen way was indeed a way of salvation for him. What they could have seen would be More's reconciliation of his whole life with his final choice, his careful examination of every possible trap into which he might have fallen, and his eventual resting of his case in God, or rather, in Christ's passion.

The more surely he proved the consistency of his actions, the more deeply he must have wounded the hearts of his family, who, though faithful in all else, had failed him in understanding and had tempted him to set aside his conscience. More's comfort for his family was a purifying fire and he cannot have been unaware of this. Yet I cannot think this his main aim, for he had long since, both in his letters and in his conversations, especially with Meg, reconciled the differences that had arisen over his actions, and their judgement of excessive scrupulosity. It seems somehow unlikely that he was setting out afresh to instruct them in discernment, detachment and the need for rigorous loyalty to truth above appearances, truth above expediency. Instead, he seems to be offering them as his last gift, and a wry one at that, a naked view of his own doubts, fears and weakness.

I doubt that More was concerned in the *Dialogue of Comfort* to seek a solution to the immediate reforming problems, or to the threat from the Great Turk to a divided Christendom. Despite the setting of the *Dialogue*, there is too much immediacy in the problems raised for me seriously to believe that More was intent upon discussing reunion. I doubt that he intended comfort for heretics in his softened attitude, since, realist that he was, he cannot have expected they would read his work. The setting in Hungary is no more the crux of the matter than the merry jests are included for merriment's sake.

For my part I cannot take to these merry jests with any feeling of gusto, even bearing in mind changing tastes in humour. Today we would call the jests black humour. Like Elton, I find them so grim as to be painful, though, unlike him, I do not object to their anti-feminine bias.[22] I do not see that as special to More. Indeed it would have been a remarkable thing if More had overcome all the anti-feminine biases of his time, and of his social traditions. No-one so deeply imbued with Augustine's writings could easily throw off that saint's Manichaean view of women and it is a bad failure in historical perspective to demand of More that he rise beyond all his age in that. After all, the *Utopia* does accept the notion of female priests.

To return to the merry jests as a source of comfort: these seem to be the product not of a misogynist, but of a man who, consistently with the vision of social reform so realistically and cogently argued in the *Utopia*, had no reason to deceive himself about the blacker recesses of human nature as he experienced it in his everyday life as lawyer, judge and courtier. Besides, in this crisis, which had resulted from the unbridled passion and wilfulness of the King, More found himself isolated from all his family, who had tossed aside his instruction and training without seeming concern for the consequences.

More knew to what dark depths human beings might fall, he knew their follies and their careless dishonesties. The merry jests could comfort no-one except by heightening the irony of More's situation as he presents it. Here he is, not a man for all seasons, but everyman, faltering on the way to heaven, his conscience at variance with that of the whole nation, courting martyrdom like the dame who provoked her husband to bring about her untimely and grisly end.[23] It seems to me that we cannot conceive how fearsome it was for More to find himself, a cautious man by legal training, if not by temperament, facing martyrdom. I do not think More was necessarily worried by the fact of martyrdom, that is by death, nor by the idea of his own martyrdom as a form of suicide. Nevertheless he must have wondered at his own temerity in manoeuvring himself into such a position when he judged himself no saint.

Though More's critics accuse him of hesitating and hedging in the face of death I think they mistake the point. More, as is apparent from his Tower letters and the *Dialogue of Comfort*, was not trying to save his life; he was trying to ensure that he was not falling into the sins of pride and presumption by rushing headlong into martyrdom. Far from being a reluctant martyr, More shows himself in the *Dialogue* to be acutely aware of the pitfalls in dying for a cause, even God's cause. The field that he assured Roper he had won on the day of his imprisonment[24] had proved to be a minor skirmish compared with the temptations on which he had leisure to reflect in the Tower. Perhaps one could conclude from the *Dialogue* that, like the monastic compilers of penitentials in an earlier age,

More's imaginings of possible sin were vastly greater than his capacity to commit them.

Not that all the temptations brought to our notice in the work are More's own; it would be foolish to think so; but there were two influences at work to produce the minute examination of variant temptations to be overcome. The first such influence is More's fiction of a young Hungarian begging advice of his wise and experienced old uncle on the course of action to be pursued in the event of an Islamic conquest and subsequent persecution of Christians.

The second influence was More's lifelong tendency to look all ways round a problem, a widely discursive habit blessedly kept in check in the economically argued *Utopia*, but apart from that, probably largely responsible for More's many unfinished works. His envisaged task frequently got beyond his time because his busy life demanded his working uneconomically on his writings, and this showed in his style and organization. Hence the sheer bulk of the *Dialogue of Comfort*. We can only be thankful that the urgency of More's own spiritual need to see his situation as clearly and as honestly as he could led him to finish the work, which otherwise might have remained a highly conceived fragment.

Even in his comfort More was austere. For one dramatic moment towards the end of the treatise, it seems to me that More allows his voice and his conclusions to coincide with those of Antony in a brief conversation of the joys of heaven.

> Howbeit yf we wold somwhat sett lesse by the filthy voluptuouse appetites of the flesh, & wold by withdrawing from them with helpe of prayour throw the grace of god, draw nere to the secret inward pleasure of the spirite, we shuld by the litle sippyng that our hartes shuld haue here now, & that sodayne tast therof/haue such an estymacion of the Incomperable & vncogitable Ioy that we shall haue (yf we will) in hevyn by the very full drawght therof/wherof it is wytten/*Satiabor quum apparuerit gloria tua*/I shalbe satyatt satisfied & fullfild whan thy glory good lord shall apere/that ys to witt with the fruytyon of the sight of goddes gloryouse maiestye face to face/ That the desire expectacion & hevenly hope therof, shall more encor-

age vs, & make vs strong to suffre & systeyne for the love of god & salvacion of our sowle/than euer we could be movid to suffre here worldly payne, by the terrible drede of all the horrible paynes that dampnid wrechys haue in hell//

Wherfor in the meane tyme for lacke of such experimentall tast, as god giveth here sometyme to some of his speciall seruauntes, to thentent we may draw toward spirituall exercise to/for which spirituall exercise/god with that gifte as with an ernest peny of there hole reward after in heven, comfortith them here in earth/Let vs not so mich with lokyng to haue describid what maner of Ioyes they shalbe, as with heryng what our lord telleth vs in holy scripture/how mervelouse greate they shalbe, labour by prayour to conceve in our hartes such a fervent longyng for them, that we may for attaynyng to them, vtterly set at nought all fleshly delight, all worldly pleasures/all erthly losses, all bodely tourment and payne/[25]

At once, however, More concludes that man is not capable of the comfort of heaven in prospect:

Howbe yt some thinges are there in scripture expressid, of the maner of the pleasures & Ioyes that we shall haue in hevin as where/*fulgebunt Iusti sicut sol, & qui erudiunt ad iustitiam tanquam scintille in arundineto discurrent*/Ryghteus men shall shyne as the sone, & shall run about like sparkes of fyre among redes//

Now tell some carnall myndid man of this maner pleasure/& he shall take litle pleasure therein, & say he careth not to haue hys flesh shyne he/nor like a sparke of fire to skyp a bowt in the skye/[26]

And so he turned to what had been the object throughout his life of his faith, his sure hope and his strongest love, the contemplation of Christ's Passion. While Mother Julian could anticipate heaven with a deep sense of reality, More's reflections were more sobering:

your adversary the devill lyke a roryng lyon, runnyth about in circuite, sckyng whome he may devoure/The devill it is therfor, that yf we for fere of men will fall, is redy to rone vppon vs & devoure vs. And it is wisedome then, so mych to thinke vppon the Turkes, that we forgete the devill/What mad man is he, that whan a lion were about to devoure hym, wold vouchsafe to regarde the bytyng of a lytle fistyng curre/Therfor whan he roreth out vppon vs by the threttes of mortall men/let vs tell hym that with our inward yie, we see hym well ynough, & intend to stand & fight with hym evyn hand to hand. Iff he thretten vs that we be to weyke/let vs tell hym that our capten Christ is with vs, & that we shall fight with his strength that hath vainquyshid hym all redy/

And let vs fence vs with fayth, & comfort vs with hope, & smyte the devill in the face with a firebrond of charitie/For surely yf we be of that tendre lovyng mynd, that our master was/& not hate them that kill vs, but pytie them & pray for them, with sorow for the perell that they work vnto them selfe/that fire of charitie throwne in his face, stryketh the devill sodaynly so blynd, that he can not see where to fasten a stroke on vs/

Whan we fele vs to bold/remembre our own feblenes/whan we fele vs to faynt/remembre Christes strength/In our fere let vs remembre Christes paynfull agonye, that hym selfe wold for our comfort suffre before his passion, to thentent that no fere shuld make vs dispayre
... that he shall ioyously bring vs to hevyn by yt (tribulation)/& than doth he much more for vs than yf he kept vs fro yt.[27]

Dialogue of comfort for whom, then? Not for everyman, unless he cast off the devil, leave aside his pusillanimity, his self-deception; not for the gamblers with salvation. More's world was not one for the gentle compassion of a Mother Julian for her even-Christians. His is the reluctant, but decisive, severity of one who knows that only a naked vision of the truth will be medicine strong enough for the ills of his time, including his own ills as well. More's comfort is costly: he alone whose treasure is in heaven can afford to buy.

Notes

1. *A Dialogue of Comfort Against Tribulation*, ed. L. L. Martz and F. Manley, vol. XII of *The Complete Works of St Thomas More* (Yale University Press, 1976), p. 279. This volume contains an excellent general introduction to the work, and an up-to-date bibliography. All footnote references will be to this edition of the *Dialogue*.
2. This is not the place to debate the opinion that More remained a firm conciliarist to the end and that there would be no incoherence in his retention of such views alongside his defence of the papacy.

3. *English Historical Review*, vol. 93, 1978, pp. 399–404.
4. Ibid., pp. 402–3. On the *Dialogue* as meditative, see the Introduction cited in note 1 above, *passim*.
5. cf. G. R. Elton, *Reform and Reformation England 1509–1558*, vol. II of *The New History of England* (London: Edward Arnold, 1977), p. 44 and n. 4.
6. cf. for example his recommendation of the *Scala Perfectionis* in his *The Confutation of Tyndale's Answer*, vol. VIII of *The Complete Works* (Yale edition), ed. L. A. Schuster, R.C. Marius, J. P. Lusardi and R. J. Schoeck, 3 vols, 1973, part 1, p. 37. For Hilton's views on the contemplative way, see *Walter Hilton's Eight Chapters on Perfection*, ed. Fumio Kuriyagawa, Studies in the Humanities and Social Relations, The Keio Institute of Cultural and Linguistic Studies, Keio University, Tokyo, 1967, *passim* but especially ch. IV.
7. For More's knowledge of Aquinas see Stapleton's *The Life and Illustrious Martyrdom of Sir Thomas More*, trans. P. E. Hallett (London: Burns and Oates, 1928), p. 38. See also the many references to Aquinas on charity in the *Dialogue*.
8. This is so constant a theme of the Tower works in particular that specific reference would give a wrong impression. Alongside the *Dialogue* there are the works formally devoted to a consideration of Christ's Passion, namely the *Treatise on the Passion* (vol. XIII of *The Complete Works*, ed. G. E. Haupt, 1976) and the *De Tristitia Christi* (vol. XIV of *The Complete Works*, ed. C. H. Miller, 1976). There is an intensified and climactic turning to the Passion from chapter 16 of the *Dialogue* to the end; cf. the Introduction by Martz and Manley, pp. cxiv-cxvii.
9. Review already cited, p. 403. For Martz and Manley's view on the autobiographical element, see especially, Introduction, section 3, 'The Self', pp. cxlvii-clxiv, and *passim*.
10. ibid., p. 401.
11. See *The Lyfe of Sir Thomas Moore, Knyghte, written by William Roper, Esquire*, ed. E. V. Hitchcock, Early English Text Society, Ordinary Series, no. 197, 1935, p. 97. The jailer was Sir William Kingston, a friend.
12. cf. More's letter to Margaret Roper, 1534, in *The Correspondence of Sir Thomas More*, ed. E. F. Rogers (Princeton University Press, 1947), Letter 210, pp. 540–4, p. 542.
13. cf. *Revelations of Divine Love*, Recorded by Julian, Anchoress at Norwich A.D. 1373, ed. and trans. G. Warrack (London: Methuen, tenth edition, 1934), Thirteenth Revelation, ch. XXVII–XL, pp. 55–83.
14. ibid., ch. XXVII, pp. 55–7.
15. ibid., ch. XXVIII, pp. 58–9.
16. ibid., ch. XXIX, p. 60.
17. ibid., ch. XL, pp. 81–2.
18. ibid., ch. XXVII, p. 55.

19. Book 1, ch. 15, pp. 46–7.
20. op. cit., ch. LXXVII, p. 188.
21. Review already cited, p. 402.
22. ibid., pp. 400–1.
23. *Dialogue*, Book II, ch. 15, p. 125.
24. Roper, op. cit., p. 73: 'the field is wonne'.
25. *Dialogue*, Book III, ch. 26, pp. 306–7.
26. ibid., p. 307.
27. ibid., Book III, ch. 27, pp. 318–9.

MORE AND SOKRATES: THE LIMITS OF COMPARISON AND SYMBOLIC POTENCY
C. & A. C. CONDREN

Among the symbolic graffiti embedded in the floor of Siena Cathedral is one of the mythical Hermes Tristmegistus conveying pagan learning to the Christian world, and one of the world under the sway of fortune, in which an unlikely looking Sokrates is being handed the palm of victory. The presence of Hermes and Sokrates in the floor of *Il Duomo* pointedly invites the reconsideration of the relationships between history and myth that pivot around the Christian awareness of pagan civilization, which ambivalently was both an encumbrance and an inheritance.

That there was a problem of relationship between, as it were, the ages of light and dark was a direct consequence of a belief in a Christian dispensation, a linear conception of time, and partly, a polemical desire to separate the pagan from the Christian.[1] On the one hand there was postulated, theologically, a fundamental gulf between the two worlds; on the other, the existence of the pagan world could hardly be theologically redundant, and there was much potentially born in the age of dark that might be of service in the light—a view that the children of *crepusculum*, such as St Augustine, could hardly avoid.

To simplify drastically, one may say that the problems raised were answered in terms of religious pragmatics. The pagan was transmitted in so far as it could be translated into Christian terms. In principle its value was a function of its figurative power and its symbolic resonance. As Petrarch had said, his studies of antiquity were made in order to bring the ancient to the feet of the modern Church.[2] Hermes on the floor, who brings wisdom by the grace of God, is himself a symbol that joins light to dark. Sokrates is perhaps the most powerful example of an ancient pagan figure becoming something of a *figura*, and something of a myth—a man becoming a representative symbol to be used variously in the light of another world.³ Christianity has hardly lacked an ability to generate symbols of its own, which, as it were, act as paradigms for the assimilation of the ancient world, the most notable species of which are the saints—people exemplifying acutely Christian ideals and providing a link between this world and the Christian afterlife. Their existence sharpens the qualities of the pagan virtuous in Christian eyes, while the pagan virtuous add a diachronic depth to the saintly class, hence the letters between St Paul and Seneca. Together the possibilities of virtue resonate across the great divide, like bright beads along a single string of time.

II

It is in this context that some general comparison between Sokrates and More, as men and as symbols, may be illuminating and not entirely arbitrary. Methodologically, however, we must try to tread a path between two extremes. At one, comparisons may easily enough become too general to have any substance. At the other, by a covert process of translation, one can easily present as a specific and direct point of comparison that which has been prejudiced or even manufactured by the terms we choose to use. Thus, for example, Edward Freeman quite properly censures Grote for translating *demagogus* as 'opposition speaker', and so employing and connoting political and institutional categories which permit purely supurious comparisons between 19th century England and ancient Athens. Again, once Emerton has rendered the term *Ciompi* as bolshevik, he has not so much uncovered a point of comparison between medieval and 20th century tyranny as manufactured a comparison through a categorical anachronism,⁴ on which dubious basis he then feels able to explain Salutati's *de Tyranno* (1400) with reference to the career of Mussolini.⁵ It is this interesting and insidious process of conceptual translation (a species of mythologizing, masquerading as comparison) that we shall meet with respect to the trials and the deaths of Sokrates and More.

A median way requires the use of a general classificatory vocabulary to which neither man is assimilated, but in terms of which each can be similarly located with respect to his own society.

Along this way there is a number of generally valid if indirect points of comparison between Sokrates and More.

i. Both men lived in societies which exhibited not singular but dual senses of political identity. Athenians, Corinthians, Spartans were all also Hellenes, and commitment to a notion of *Hellas* could cut across loyalto to *polis*, its rhetoric channelling and justifying what might also be seen as the fermentation of *stasis*. Commitment to *polis* was always a fragile plant, torn at its roots by family and locality, at its branches by a sense of Hellenic identity. Similarly, an Englishman or an Italian was also a member of Christendom, recognition of which could, as it did with Becket, qualify allegiance to *regnum*. So too, the rhetoric of the peace of Christendom could cloak family and local aspirations that could tear at the fabric of society. Sokrates' sense of identity as an Athenian was probably misunderstood, qualified less than his accusers feared; More's qualified loyalty to his prince was understood too well.

ii. Both men, as needs no labouring, had an uncompromising sense of moral absolutism, a not uncommon phenomenon, but particularly significant when we note that both lived in societies in which the received moral vocabularies were unstable. Sokrates lived through the period in which the inherited moral vocabulary of Homer's world and archaic Greece was collapsing, and beginning to be replaced by a new range of moral sensibilities, requiring a transformed moral and political language.[6] More's situation was similar; there is a sense of the decadent and a depressing foreboding that permeates much of the writing of the late 15th and early 16th centuries, which has improperly surprised some historians blinded by such labels as 'the renaissance', the 'rise of the modern state', 'the age of discovery'.[7] But this sense of decline, not of the middle ages, of course, but of Christendom, was well founded, Christendom seemed to be fragmenting and to be externally threatened; no longer the world, it was struggling to maintain its place within the world.[8] A perceptive pessimism is found in thinkers who parenthesize More's life: in Aeneas Sylvius Piccolomini's famous letter to Rome of 1454 lamenting the lack of loyalty to church and empire alike; and a generation later in the astrologer Pomponatius's belief in the imminent collapse of Christianity itself. The so-called rise of the modern state was in effect the collapse of Christendom, it replaced a dual with a singular sense of political identity, and with it came a change in the vocabulary of politics. Indeed, like the collapse of the Homeric honour code, which could not survive the emergence of the classical *polis*, this collapse was principally one of moral and political vocabulary which abridged Christendom's sense of purpose and the qualities of political life: a ring of *cles mots* unable to open the doors of political appraisal.

If Sokrates stands between the old Homeric honour code and the new co-operative conception of the *polis* intimated by the great tragedians and defined by Plato and Aristotle, More may be seen as standing between the *regna* of Christendom and the European state intimated by Machiavelli and defined by Hobbes. As we are dealing with ethico-political conceptions, both Sokrates and More are better located with respect to linguistic rather than institutional change. In such periods of conceptual transformation, a sense of the morally absolute is apt to look out of touch, and is certainly difficult to maintain in that the very elements of moral discussion are too often unstable. Sokrates and Gorgias, More and Machiavelli, share parallel communities of different problems. Further, both Sokrates and More drew on parallel aspects of their inheritances in order to maintain some sense of the absolute. Sokrates drew on an inheritance of the importance of the oracles and possibly shamanistic wisdom in evoking his notion of the *daimonion*—the inner voice. More's behaviour and sense of moral purpose came from his belief in a knowable Christian God whose purposes for mankind were mediated through the head of Christendom. Both, in short, relied upon similarly universal contexts of their political identities in order to express a sense of moral absolutism with respect to the possibilities of proper action.

iii. It is not surprising that both appear to have shared similarly ambivalent attitudes to political activity, though both were very much political animals. Sokrates, as citizen of Athens, was perforce a political animal, in the only way that made sense to the Athenians. When called upon he performed his probouleutic duties, the very proof of his being *eleutheros*. He was, however, by no means totally committed to the politics of his society, as both Plato and his accusers make clear. The political arena was not the only, or necessarily the most suitable, stage on which man should exhibit his virtues. If the arena was inescapable and the most natural setting for the *agathos*, it also provided a constant source of corruption. As Sokrates is made to lament in *The Republic* (a latish work, but the comment seems in character), how much more dangerous is man of philosophic potential if corrupted by his political society.[11] In Shakespeare's image, 'lilies that fester smell far worse than weeds'. If More's society afforded something of a genuine choice concerning political participation, More's own decision to hazard the life at court was patently marked by ambivalence. For men of More's world, the possibilities of apolitical citizenship clearly pointed the character of political life, especially life in the ambit of a Prince.

In a world of monasteries and universities one could hardly be an unselfconscious political citizen. Thus the familiar *topoi* and maxims of the ancient world concerning politics and moral corruption had different points for Sokrates and More, the *Epigrammata* are translations in at least two senses of the word. If he did not like the heat, the citizen *could* leave the hothouse. Equally few were called to enter a world of rapid growth and sudden decay, wherein the King's displeasure could signal death.[12] Lilies could fester, lilies could bloom, and this was precisely why the good man should make the effort to enter courtly life. For the good man to quit the hothouse, despite the dangers of death and corruption, the whole world became a worse place. Such grounds were shared possibly by Machiavelli, certainly later by Clarendon.[13] But if the grounds were plausible enough, lacking a Guicciardini's praise of ambition as a political virtue, they could be little more than a covert justification for self-seeking, and self-deception, and there may be just a touch of such self-deception in More, as there was in Clarendon when he tried to serve too many masters for too long.[14] But if both More and Sokrates shared ambivalent attitudes to political activity and the dangers of corruption, their awarenesses can hardly have had the same metaphysical grounding. For only in a Christian, post-Augustinian world is political life necessarily entangled with human corruption, politics having no *finalis intentio* is a product of the expulsion from Eden, and by augmenting the temptations of private life is doubly dangerous for the fallen. For a Sokrates such beliefs would seem absurd, but for all the inheritors of the conception of Christendom, such as More and Machiavelli, they provided the *a priori* warning that needed fleshing out only with historical examples.

iv. Given a superficially similar but differently rooted political ambivalence, it is not surprising that both More and Sokrates can easily be read as critics of their respective societies. Xenophon notwithstanding, Sokrates's life and death are unintelligible except as sustained acts of social criticism. More, from his fanciful exploration of tyranny in the *Richard*, to his imaginative fear that sheep will eat men, was a critic of the society to which he was also committed.

Further, with both, the force and direction of their criticisms are somewhat elusive. For Sokrates this is principally the case because he did not write but was interpreted through his diverse followers and critics.

We can do little better than explore the compound image created each for his own purposes by Aristophanes, Xenophon and Plato; of direct evidence there is none. With More the elusiveness is the result of his mode of writing—his persistent, perhaps his deliberately defensive indirection[15] Thus with the *Epigrammata* the points at which More speaks and More seeks to translate are often obscure. With the *Richard* and the

Utopia, the general categories of time and geographical space are used to achieve a potential distance between the written works and the force of what More has to say.[16] Disingenuous perhaps, cautious certainly, and from this arises an ambiguity, like the *de facto* ambiguity of the evidence surrounding the real Sokrates, which results in a diversity of possibility for interpretation and use. Underlying the symbolic resonance of each man is a fruitful ambiguity.

We may, however, go a little further; More, it seems, had an unambiguous respect for law and custom, and so too apparently did Sokrates. Richard's disrespect is one of the principal marks of the tyrant, the Utopians' respect for law *per se* one of their unquestionable virtues. But here there is a danger. We must be careful not to convert this respect into clear evidence for a shared social conservatism. More lived in a world in which the rhetoric of law and custom was *de rigeur*; even the most revolutionary of statutes (*Quia Emptores,* the *Constitutions of Clarendon* and the *Acts of Succession and Supremacy*) were all defensible in terms of custom. Whatever a man respected he could justify through the idiom of custom, whatever he abhorred could be its breach. Custom and law were thus highly prescriptive terms, they were a part of every apologist's armoury. That More in fact lived in a period of considerable legal change merely complicates our problems of understanding.

Again the parallel with Sokrates is pointed but indirect. He lived in a similarly confusing period of legal change, and if we are to be guided by Plato's earliest dialogues, espoused an absolutist respect for the forms of law. This respect, however, would have been grounded less in a sense of tradition transmitted over time than in a belief that *nomos* was embedded in a vibrant *physis*. During Sokrates's lifetime, however, the precise scope of *nomos* and its relationship to *physis* were both matters of doubt—and there appears to have been something of a free-floating rhetoric of *physis* and *nomos* as there was of custom and law in More's time. In short, in times of legal transition both could still call on rhetorics of legal establishment, and it is thus perhaps less ironic than it might seem that both, more or less through due process of law, were tried and executed.

III

Thus far we have outlined some general lines along which the comparison of figures such as Sokrates and More can proceed: that is, given a general classificatory vocabulary, we can, as it were, delineate a set of parallel taxonomies. But to repeat: this process of indirect comparison is not to be confused with seeing Sokrates and More as sharing the same problems, confronting the same issues and ideas, being in the same camp, being prominent beads on the same string. There is a difference between a vocabulary deployed to get to grips with a variety of problems, and the reduction of any one set of problems to the terms of another.

It is this particular confusion which is a great temptation in dealing with that which seems to provide the most obvious and significant point of comparison between the two men—the meaning and underlying issues of their trials and deaths.

What we understand to be the common conspectus may be abridged as follows. Both Sokrates and More were public men of high moral principle whose consciences required them in the name of a higher law to refuse to do what the authority of the state demanded. Both, as Wilde might have put it, played Antigone to different Creons in the name of liberty, conscience and the moral order. As neither would compromise, both were tried, and with the aid of perjury, malice and dubious charges, were similarly condemned, and died upholding their principles, despite the attempts of others to persuade them to comply with the requirements of the state.

All this seems to be very plausible, but a large part of its plausibility arises through shifting from general classificatory categories to a community of specific issues, which were not Sokrates's, nor strictly speaking More's, but are rather ours, in terms of which the trials of both men may be translated to make common and reassuring sense to us.

Our own political experience is characterized by a distinctive vocabulary that provides the problems in terms of which we see political action, the criteria of political judgement, and an attendant rhetoric of political eristics. It functions somewhat, though not so neatly, as our received field of chromatic discrimination divides our palette into the spectrum of colours through which we appraise the hues and tincture of the world around us.

A large part of the political field of terms is constituted by such reciprocally related *clés mots* as *conscience, authority, state freedom, public, private, right* and *obligation*. To use this vocabulary is to be engaged in some form of political speculation. What we must remember, however, is the historical contingency of both the political and chromatic fields of terms we nowadays normally employ. Between the 16th and 20th centuries there have been changes both subtle and significant, though as is usually the way with language, none have been easily discernible, nor predictable in their ramifications. New words have come into political prominence (state, nation, totalitarian); old words have fallen into political desuetude (loyalty, custom, piety); and continuingly significant terms have greatly changed in denotation, connotation and emotional resonance (democracy, rhetoric, right, conscience and class).

We are not saying here that, for example, people are no longer loyal, pious and so forth, but that the vocabulary through which issues are formulated and the political world is understood, has changed, not totally, but significantly; not with respect to individual words acting as independent variables, some of which may retain some permanent residue of fixed meaning, but with respect to a whole reciprocally related field of terms.[17] And if the language that structures political discourse and awareness has changed between More's world and ours, we can hardly hold our political problems in common. These points, however, are easily overlooked because of the superficial continuity of many terms between the 16th century and now, and because of the positive desire to press the past into the shape of the present. The floundering world of 16th century Christendom may thus easily be translated into the terms that characterize the modern industrial nation-state, a process of translation that is categorically anachronistic, and systematically distorting; for any account of More's trial that trades in terms of *state, individual* and *conscience* (in a modern sense) delineates the political world and its problems as More never did. At the beginning of the 16th century 'state' was hardly a part of western political vocabulary, 'family' and functional 'class' were more significant abstractions than 'individual', and 'conscience'—a word much favoured by More—was by no means clearly everybody's right of appeal, any more than it was unequivocally a witness to a fact, or alternatively a judge of right or almost on occasions an opinion or view that could simply be changed.[18] Indeed, before the term came to refer uniformly to everyone's belief as to what it was right for them to do as individuals, it hardened into the very different Miltonic sign of an infallible and exclusive moral knowledge.[19] In short, of the main meanings found in the 16th century, one achieved a dominance in the 17th century, and the other, in a very extended sense, has become normal in the 20th century. When More spoke of his conscience, we cannot be certain he entertained our meaning of the word, but we can be sure that he was aware of meanings we have all but forgotten, in a very different context of lexical associations, and that it did not assume the importance we have much later attached to it.[20] Thus the recent acknowledgement by the Anglican Church that More is one who died for conscience' sake would seem to have more ecumenical charity than historical validity: his virtue thus becomes unquestionable without evoking problematic connotations of Roman authority.

With Sokrates the continuities are even more severely fractured. Between him and More were interposed the civilizations of Rome and Christendom, and we now employ terms that owe much to both and little or nothing to Greece. The notions of public and private, power and authority, we owe to Roman political awareness, those of redress and representation largely to medieval Christian society.

Indeed the field of political terms with which the Greek was at home is now remarkably alien to us. Notions of pollution, appearance, personal honour, impiety, courage and cunning were of paramount importance. Justice, until Plato, had an uncertain status;[21] there was no clear concept of authority;[22] the notions of freedom and representation were almost the reverse of our understandings;[23] and a notion of individual moral responsibility seems to have been quite absent.[24] In this context there is certainly no place for a conscience in a modern sense, and Sokrates's *daimonion* is none such. Lewis quite properly does not associate *daimonion* with conscience, his starting points in Greek being *oida* (I know) and *sunoida* (I share knowledge with). Liddell and Scott's *Lexicon* circumscribes the area of reference for *daimonion* as divine operation, and associates *daimonia* with a lesser class of demons. *Genius*, in the Latin sense, is probably closer than conscience. Ironically, when Tertullian understood the Sokratic *daimonion* to be a form of demon, and contrasted all such *daemonia* with Christian wisdom, he was, despite his apologetic motivation, much closer to the historical and linguistic truth than the contemporary association of *daimonion* with conscience.[25] Similarly, it is little wonder that we search in vain in Plato's account of Sokrates's trial and death for a satisfying defence of individual freedom from the authority of the state, or conversely for a doctrine of unqualified obedience to what it decrees. It is more wondrous that we continue to look.[26]

Because Homer wrote of wine dark seas flowing black blood and other fancies, when we all know that the sea is but occasionally red with blood, and for all its effects wine is never blue, grey or green, it has been held that the Greeks were colour blind. What is overlooked is that the Greek chromatic field was not ours, nor its discriminations replicas of ours by any other set of names.[27] That is true, though more clearly of Attic political vocabulary at the time of Sokrates's death; it is true, though less completely, of English political vocabulary at the time of More's. To equate the issues of Sokrates's fate with More's, and both with our problems, and the issues defined by our language, is to suffer a sort of conceptual colour blindness, to perpetrate a chromatic reductionism, a grey on grey, which is the mark of historical blindness. Above all it is the mark not of historical interpretation but of symbolic elaboration and translation, and it is in this respect above all else that More and Sokrates may be directly compared.

In ceasing to be living men with their own experiences and problems, they both became symbols, passive coins in the exchange and reckonings of others. But this general point itself needs cashing, the term symbol unpacking, to which end we propose to make use of Frye's nomenclature of symbolism, which suggests a strikingly similar location for both Sokrates and More.[28]

IV

Frye identifies a symbol minimally as any unit of a literary structure which can be isolated for critical attention, and for which we are required to admit multilayered meaning. He further refines symbols as motifs and signs, images, archetypes and finally monads.[29]

At the most specific and contextually simple level, motifs are the abridgements of relationships between literary phenomena contained within the context of literary occurrence; signs are similar abridgements but with direct reference to the extrinsic world. Thus, for example, Cummings's characteristic lower-case letters are motifs; the letters St before More's name a sign. The distinctions reflect the common linguistic one between primary and secondary contexts, and at a further remove, the distinction between coherence and correspondence as criteria for truth. We assess the distribution of a sign in terms of its correspondence with some aspect of the extrinsic world, of a literary motif in terms of its coherence with other aspects of the literary artefact.

Images are modifications of motifs—significant metaphors, similies or allegories, which stand for or encapsulate a potentially wide range of ideas that require some decoding, such as the towers in Yeats's poetry, which stand for altogether more than they explicitly suggest.

Archetypes are in turn modifications of images, those that form part of the common literary inheritance of a specific civilization, conveying much the same range of associations within it. Thus the imaginary blood on Lady Macbeth's hands, an image within a play, is also part of a widely shared associational field for blood, red and guilt, which gives rise to such expressions as being caught red-handed. Archetypes provide, as it were, a stable, well-worn literary currency of a civilization. Finally, monads are those archetypes that function cross-culturally, sharing similar or parallel sorts of associations in different civilizations. Monadic symbolism was the sort that Coleridge was referring to when he spoke of the imagination creating images.[30] Thus light and dark are almost universally images of good and evil, knowledge and ignorance[31] –though what may be subsumed under these less pictorial terms may vary considerably [32]

Now there is a great deal that could be said about Frye's symbolic continuum, but in the context of this paper the following points may be stressed.

i. At all points the symbols are not mere ornamentation; they are a means of imposing some conceptual order upon the world, of structuring and conveying some sense of structure to the reader, often when confronting the difficult. MacLeish once remarked, with respect to his own use of the image of Job, 'When you are dealing with questions too large for you, which, nevertheless, will not leave you alone, you are obliged to house them somewhere.'[33] Symbols house and help aid the formulation and delineation of the world's problems and possibilities, supplementing, at times personifying, the more abstract fields of terms used to similar ends.

Thus the archaic Greeks used a genealogical relationship between the goddesses *Themis* and *Dike* to house an understanding of the ideal relationship between *themistes* (ordinances) and *dikaiasune*.[34] And it was this ability to shift from the purely symbolic and poetic ordering of the world to an abstract conceptualization of it that Vico saw as marking the limits of the primitive and the rational mind.

ii. Frye depicts his continuum as parallel with the principal modes of interpretation that Aquinas discusses in the *Summa Theologiae*[35]—thus it provides not so much exlusive categories as a range of terms appropriate to different kinds of understanding; a monadic symbol may provide motifs. It might also be seen, however, as a continuum of increasing contextual complexity, and of decreasing intension of meaning, factors that suggest, as it were, the axes for plotting symbolic significance.

iii. The more widely available and freely used established symbols are, the less they have specific force, the ability to delineate or abridge any uniformly precise understanding. Concomitantly, however, they gain greatly in extensive, if vague, suggestiveness. The use of such hallowed if vague symbols in practical and religious discourse is common and not merely soporific. It identifies speaker and audience with an apparently shared experience and awareness (what makes a cliche being mutual familiarity), in which process of identification the deft manipulation and co-option of resonant symbols are a principal rhetorical strategy.

Now if we seek to locate More and Sokrates in terms of the above, we find their positions are strikingly similar. Both can be seen to function at all symbolic levels, and in both cases this is a function of similarly archetypal or monadic status.

First, Sokrates as symbol is certainly monadic, More arguably so, depending on just where and according to what criteria one draws the lines between distinctive civilizations.

Secondly, they function in the same symbolic nexus, within the world of political and moral discourse, they house the same sorts of problems, they personify the same cluster of contemporary abstract world-ordering conceptions—integrity, individuality, humanity, principled self-sacrifice and wisdom—the individual on the side of rights versus the state. This means more than just that they are both personifications of 'good' as opposed to 'evil'. They are both symbols ranged against the potential misuse of political authority, figures at the gates of a higher moral realm. They are thus symbols less available to established authority than to those who wish to identify with the subjects of the state's authority, or who wish to stress that authority's responsibility. Consequently, the simple association of Sokrates and/or More with a contemporary situation, say involving conscientious objection, the persecution of intellectuals or dissent on religious grounds, evokes an immensely resonant inheritance. Thus when they are used as symbols, the writer is writing not about them but about the present, trailing a coat of suitably lineal colours—a situation that often requires scant decoding because of such expressions as 'we have a lot to learn from the life of . . .' or 'the death of . . . is a warning to us all'. This we suggest may help explain why politicians have been (despite sometimes uncertain knowledge) so willing to speak on More over the last two celebratory years. They praise the symbol and thereby identify themselves with the qualities it houses, and the audiences who hold it dear. In trading in a traditional symbolic currency they make a sort of down-payment on political respectability —there but for the Grace of God go all politicians of integrity. We cannot imagine a similar willingness to talk on Hobbes or (outside Italy) on Machiavelli.

Thirdly, if both are typically tokens in the currency of moral and political discourse, there are similar barriers in the way of making either effective literary symbols, and in the way of untangling the historical truth about them.

The dead weight of moralizing cliche is apt to limit their literary potential—to adopt a thoroughly aestheticist position, moral investment is an enemy of art.[36] It is true that Plato was able to make Sokrates a figure of considerable literary power in his early dialogues, but then the mythical Sokrates was still to be defined; Plato achieved this and it was above all his work which defined Sokrates as a *topos* for future reference— one taken up by Demosthenes and his rival Aeschines, for example, and possibly even the writers of the Greek New Testament, who may have made aeretological use of Sokrates in their accounts of the crucifixion of Christ.[37] Certainly the possible association of Sokrates and Christ were given brilliant, if brief, expression by Voltaire, who called Christ the Sokrates of Galilee. But the Sokratic image is usually more banal. When Graves sees the hemlock as a poison fit for a male chauvinist, one finds only an ingenious flippancy,[38] and when Fowles speaks of Sokrates as the philosopher who preferred hemlock to the lie,[39] only a tired vulgarization of a now age-old and well-worn cliche.[40]

Even more has St Thomas been mewed up in the clichaic realms of moral enthusiasm; the didactic invariably triumphs over the poetic; the play *St Thomas More* is virtually an unperformed item of Shakespearian apocrypha, *A Man for All Seasons* a noble failure.

That moral investment in both has hampered historical understanding of either can be seen in a number of ways. The reactions of 18th and 19th (and even some 20th) century classicists to the death of Sokrates is a fair guide to their opinions about the French and American revolutions and/or modern democracy; while with respect to More one might ask only, why the quincentenary celebrations? But further, if, as Professor Elton would have us believe, More was sexually unbalanced, there is no shortage of those who would reject his views, and not only because of the lack of firm historical evidence. Or when Sir Clements Markham argued that More was a dishonest historian, a historiographical reaction is the last thing one gets. One gets reactions less appropriate to historical activity than to actions of libel. The image is more important to many than the man, which has not proved an abundant help to scholarship.

There is a sense in which, with respect to both, we are living almost, at times, in a pre-Darwinian universe, one in which the truths of religion appear to be balanced on the shoulders of Adam; but if Adam did not exist, or if he stands upon an elephant, and the elephant upon a turtle; if, that is, the received images of Sokrates and More are not firmly embedded in truth, and if the men buried beneath did not share our problems, there are too many who think that the standards and certainties of the present are thus challenged.

With respect to both men's symbolic significance, the differences, as Frye's nomenclature would suggest, are only of degree, and their status is supplementary. Sokrates has been in use for much longer, transcending the age of darkness, not least because he was blessed with a mythographer of talent and disciple of surpassing genius. More has been used less extensively, but with an intensity with which few other such well-established symbols can compare. A synthesis of the two would give us a figure of the potency of Christ, in whose shadow, in their different ways, both stand. But the fusion of the two is not entirely at one remove; there is a sense in which a Sokratic image of himself may well stand behind the *Dialogue of Comfort*; a Platonic image stands behind the mythography of Roper.[41] The reports of the conversations in the Tower aimed at persuading More to change his 'conscience' and make his peace with his king may have been consciously modelled on Plato's dramatic account of Crito's equally unsuccessful attempts in the cell to persuade Sokrates not to die,[42] while in the reports of their final crises both Sokrates and More are seen to comfort their comforters—Crito and Sir William Kingston.[43] If this is so, one reason why the historical Sokrates and the historical More seem so comparable is that the Sokratic symbol, embedded in the floor of the church, was already available as a housing for the problems that in his final months would not leave More alone, and that could add such resonance to the cries of his apologists. Harpsfield's testimony is enough:

> O noble and worthy voice of our noble, new, Christian Socrates! The old Socrates, the excellent virtuous philosopher, was also unjustly put to death; whom, when his wife, at that time following, outrageously cried, 'Shall such a good man be put to death?' 'Peace, good wife,' quoth he, 'and content theyself; it is far better for me to die a good and true man than as a wretched malefactor to live.'[44]

Notes

1. Gerald A. Press, 'History and the Development of the Idea of History in Antiquity', in *History & Theory*, 16 (1977), no. 3, pp. 281–96. Compare also Joseph Levinson, *Confucian China and Its Modern Fate*, chapter 3, vol. III (Routledge & Kegan Paul, London, 1965) on the separation of past and present in modern China, and his conclusion, especially pp. 113–15, where an early Christian parallel is drawn.
2. Cited J. Huizinga, *Men and Ideas*, trans. J. S. Holmes and Hans van Marle, Meridian, New York, 1965, pp. 273.
3. The evidence of the use of Sokrates in the ancient world is patchy, but it appears to have been both persistent and varied—a vital means by which men came to terms with their troublesome inheritance. Quintilian and Cicero make extensive use of him; he loomed large in Stoic and Cynic pedigrees; he was widely used by Christian writers, most notably Jerome, Augustine, Tertullian and John Chrysostom; and he was available equally for apostate polemic- see Libanius, *De Socratis Silentio, (Opera,* E.J.R. Forster, vol. V, Stuttgart 1909). In English, much valuable documentation is provided by John Ferguson, *Socrates: A Source Book*, Macmillan, London, 1970.
4. For further comment and more formal elaboration see C. Condren, 'An Historiographical Paradox', in F. McGregor & N. Wright, eds., *European History and its Historians*, Adelaide University Union Press, Adelaide, 1977, p. 86.
5. Freeman, *Historical Essays*, Second Series, London, 1800, p. 154; E. E. Emerton, *Humanism and Tyranny*, Peter Smith, Glos., Mass., 1964, pp. 53 and 63 respectively.
6. See at length, A. W. H. Adkins, *Merit and Responsibility*, Oxford University Press, 1962.
7. e.g., M. Gilmore, *The World of Humanism*, Harper, New York, 1952, pp. 1–4.
8. This was the main significance of the term 'Europe' being extended from the esoteric realms of cartography to those of social and political awareness. It was only as Christendom failed as an abridgement of political experience that the term 'Europe' took on political reference. See Denys Hay, *Europe, The Emergence of an Idea*, Edinburgh University Press, 1955.
9. Quoted in Gilmore, op. cit., p. 1.
10. Cited in C. S. Lewis, *A History of English Literature in the 16th Century excluding Drama*, Oxford University Press, 1973, p. 5.
11. *Republic*, 495a.
12. 'And so they said that these matters be Kings' games, as it were, stage plays, and for the more part played upon scaffolds, in which the poor men be but the lookers-on' (*The History of King Richard III*, R. S. Sylvester, Yale, 1976, p. 83). The pun on scaffold is vital here. Adages concerning the uncertainty of life of men in public

politics were common; Roper cites one:'Indignatis principis mors est' (Life of Sir Thomas More, Knight, in E. E. Reynolds, *Lives of St Thomas More*, Dent, London, 1963, p. 35), and More's *Epigrammata* sporadically explore the theme.

13. *Il Principe*, 22 and 23. For Clarendon, see *Contemplations and Reflexions on the Psalms*, on which see I. Coltman, *Public Men and Private Causes*, Faber, London, 1962, especially parts I and II. The theme is perhaps ultimately rooted in Plato, e.g., *Rep.* 519C–8.
14. Coltman, ibid., pp. 116–21.
15. On More's intellectual caution and indirection see D. J. Grace, *The Political Thought of St Thomas More, 1509–1521*, unpublished Ph. D. thesis, University of New South Wales.
16. So too with the *Dialogue of Comfort*, but with this and the other works mentioned, the indirection also functions to disperse and augment his points of reference beyond England—a direct consequence of More's dual sense of political identity. G. Elton makes this point with respect to the *Dialogue* in reviewing the Yale edition of *The Tower Works* in *English Historical Review*, April 1978.
17. The problem is not, strictly speaking, one of whether human nature has changed (as e.g., Erwin Panowsky would have it) but a question of how it is conceptualized and appraised.
18. C. S. Lewis, *Studies in Words*, Cambridge University Press, 1974, p. 181f, who discusses the first two senses at length. For all three of these, at times bewildering, senses of the term, see the letter from Margaret Roper to Alice Alington (August 1534), item 206 in *Correspondence of Sir Thomas More*, ed. E. F. Rogers, (Princeton, N. J. 1947, and Books for Libraries, N. Y. 1970).
19. Milton, *Areopagetica*, a fine discussion of which is to be found in W. Kendall, 'How to Read Milton's *Areopagitica*', in *The Journal of Politics*, vol. XXII, 1960, pp. 439–73.
20. Lewis, op. cit., pp. 202–4.
21. Adkins, op. cit., at length.
22. J. L. Myers (*The Political Ideas of the Greeks*, Greenwood, New York, 1967, p. 142) remarks that it could refer to the end of a piece of rope, a cause, a foundation, a beginning, as well as referring to public office and to initiation.
23. Representation was the mark of the slave. On *eleutheria* see Myers, ibid, p. 319f.
24. This, and its consequences for understanding Greek society, is Adkins's starting point. His position here is hardly idiosyncratic among classical scholars, especially those concerned with the understanding of Greek Tragedy, but it is a position we do well to ignore, or consider to be free of any significant repercussions, whenever we wish to appropriate the Greeks to ourselves.
25. Lewis, op. cit., p. 181. Tertullian, *De Anima*, ed. J. H. Waszink, Amsterdam, 1947, I. 2–6. For Waszink's detailed notes, see pp. 83–98. See also Tertullian, *Apology*, XXII 1–3, and Minucius

Felix, *Octavius*, XXIV.9, who writes of the command and will *(ad natum et arbitrium)* of Sokrates's attendant/besieging demon, *(adsidentis sibi daemonis)*. Such an association is blithely asserted, e.g., by C. J. Friedrich, *An Introduction to Political Theory*, Harper & Row, New York, 1967, p. 86.

26. See, e.g., Rex Martin, 'Socrates on Disobedience to Law', in *The Review of Metaphysics*, 24, 1970, pp. 21–38, and also references to p. 21.
27. Consider the term *glaukon*, which covered the chromatic range light blue, grey, green, greyish green. It could also mean bright and gleaming.
28. N. Frye, *Anatomy of Criticism*, Princeton University Press, 1975, 2nd essay: 'Ethical Criticism: Theory of Symbols', pp. 71–128.
29. ibid., Introduction, pp. 71–3.
30. Coleridge, *Biographia Literaria*, ch. 13. Coleridge speaks of the primary imagination as the agent of perception, and the secondary as idealizing and ordering this perception; both are essentially creative.
31. C. S. Lewis remarks in *The Allegory of Love* (Galaxy, New York, 1964, p. 44) that it is more sensible to ask how these associations became severed than to try and trace their initial joining.
32. Consider Plato's imagery of the cave, and the difficulties of unravelling precisely what he wished to convey by it, and the ease with which it could be made to subsume Christian notions that were expressed in similar imagery.
33. Archibald MacLeish, cited in *Myth and Symbol*, ed. Berenice Slote, University of Nebraska Press, 1963, p. 79.
34. On these relationships, see Myers, op. cit., p. 183.
35. Aquinas, *Summa Theologiae*, Ia, Iae, 10, reply to question 3.
36. Here 'aestheticist' needs some unpacking. We are not referring to aestheticism as a rule of conduct for life (*à la* Walter Pater, and Wilde ambivalently), which is itself a moral position. Here aestheticism refers to certain standards and vocabulary (concerning form, style, unity of image, metre etc.) which are logically distinguishable from moral categories of appraisal, and which are the means by which we assess phenomena as artistic constructs *per se*. The danger, then, that moral judgement brings is that of intellectual confusion as to which standards of appraisal we wish to apply in the consideration of an artefact.
37. H. C. Kee, *Jesus in History*, Harcourt Brace Jovanovich, New York, 1970, p. 121.
38. R. Graves, *The White Goddess*, Faber, London, 1962, p. 11.
39. John Fowles, *Daniel Martin*, Little Brown & Co., Boston, 1977, p. 178.
40. Boethius (*The Consolation of Philosophy*, Book I, 3, 15–20, 30–35) makes the appropriate allusions in the context of asking of his own fate whether this is the first time that wisdom has been exposed by the wicked (*improbos*) to ruin/death (*periculis*). The

graffito in which Sokrates is handed the palm of victory may contain an allusion to Boethius's comment concerning Sokrates's victory over an unjust death. See also Tertullian, *Apology*, XIV, 7; and Ferguson, op. cit., p. 30, who cites Origen, *Against Celsius*, 9.7.

41. Consider the question of More's second wife, Lady Alice, whose reputation on very little evidence is that of a shrew treated with tolerant amusement by her husband. The character is beautifully drawn in Roper. Harpsfield (*Life and Death* ... ed. E. E. Reynolds, Dent, London 1963, p. 107) calls her 'aged, blunt and rude', and provides some suitably shrewish dialogue. Sokrates also allegedly had two wives, the second of whom, Xanthippe, had a reputation for shrewish bad temper, and who was treated with tolerant amusement by Sokrates when, as some said, he could not get out of her way (see especially the *Socrates* of Diogenes Laertius). The similarities could just be coincidence, but it seems possible that the character of More's wife is something of a myth modelled on a Xanthippean image, to extend and refine the image of More himself. (J. H. Marsden, *Philomorus*, London, 1878, p. 56, writes of Alice playing Xanthippe to More's Sokrates.) Certainly Jerome's anecdote from Diogenes Laertius (cited Ferguson, op. cit., p. 312) could fit both couples. After abusing Sokrates at length, Xanthippe finally poured dirty water over him. 'He simply dried his head, saying, "I always knew there would be rain after all that thunder" ' (*Against Jovinianus*, I.48). The anecdote was much cited throughout the 16th century. See Sir John Harington, *The Metamorphosis of Ajax*, ed. Elizabeth S. Donno, London 1962, p. 153, where the rain is appropriately the contents of a chamber pot, and fn 254 for other uses. This matter is further discussed in C. Condren. 'Dame Alice More as Xanthippe', in *Moreana*, 64, 1980, pp. 59–64.

42. See the letter from Margaret Roper to Alice Alington (1534) in *Correspondence*, op. cit., which Chambers thinks might even have been written by More, and in which Margaret seems clearly cast in the role of Crito.

43. Compare the opening passages of Plato's *Crito*, especially Crito's breaking the news to Sokrates of the arrival of the ship from Delos, with Roper: 'In good faith, Master Roper, I was ashamed of myself, that, at my departing from your father, I found my heart so feeble, and his so strong, that he was fain to comfort me, which should rather have comforted him.' William Roper, *Life of Sir Thomas More Knight*, ed. E.E. Reynolds, op. cit., p. 47.

44. Harpsfield, *Life and Death* ..., p. 164.